LIFE: ANOTHER FOUR-LETTER WORD

My True Story of Abuse, Addiction, Prison and Freedom

Bryon Sullivent

TULSA, OKLAHOMA

DECEMBER 2017

DEDICATION

Every once in a while, you will meet someone who will change the way you see the world. For me, that person is Phil. So, for that reason, I am dedicating this story to him. Thanks, Phil!

INTRODUCTION

The story you are about to read is true. Before you get into it, I feel you should know that there was much more to my life than what is shared here. Not every moment of my life was horrible, nor was I able to share all the horrible things about my life. What I did share were the larger, more powerful events that were pivotal turning points. I also didn't go into each chapter with a desire to draw needless graphic images with my words.

It is not my intention to glorify any of the illegal things that I speak of in the story. I also do not speak of anyone mentioned here in a slanderous way. Everyone mentioned was a person that I encountered as I made my way through this journey called life. What I am sharing is meant to be about me, and how the people, places, and things that I encountered affected my life.

As you read, I want to remind you that no matter how bad you may think that my life has been, there are so many people out there who have had it much, much worse. So, if you believe that God answers prayers, I ask you to pray for them.

CHAPTER 1: THE TRAGEDY OF LIFE

As I begin to tell this story, there is something you should know first.

"The tragedy of life is not death, it is what we let die inside while we live!"

My story begins on August 11, 1964. I was born to parents that had no business being married, let alone having children. Nonetheless, there I was, a healthy baby boy with no hate in my heart, no anger, no prejudice, and no ability to talk.

I have no real memories of life at this young age, I only know what happened by listening to stories much later in my life. Although I can't prove it, I'm sure that all the drama that took place in those early years, was a direct result of my being born and ruining both of my parents' lives.

My father was in the Army, so we moved around a lot when I was baby. My mother looked after me and played the role of house wife. This went on till I was three years-old. My father was sent to Germany, and my mom and I joined him there a month or so later. We moved into an apartment off-base. It is here that I have my first real memories as a child, and it is here that I first began to die inside.

My mother was pregnant with my soon-to-be little sister. So, it was hard for her to care for me in her condition. The first memory I have of my own was of my mom sending me to fetch groceries at the mom-and-pop store on the other side of a large wooded area outside of our apartment. She gave me a list and money and I would grab my sled and mittens and head out. When I got to the market the nice people there would fill a box with the items on the list and tie it to my sled. Then the women would let me pick a pastry to eat on my way home from a display case by the front door. Pastry in hand, and sled in tow, I made my way back to the apartment. It was on one of these trips that I happened to come home to my parents arguing. I mean having a knock down drag out fight. So, there I was, three years-old, holding a box of groceries, listening to them screaming at each other through the door. I stood there crying, scared to open the door for fear of what I might find. Don't forget, we were in Germany, I barely spoke English.

I had no one to run to for help and couldn't explain anything to them if I had had someone. This is when I learned of fear and helplessness. The innocence of youth had begun to die on this day which was March 24, 1968. How could I possibly know that, you ask? Well, let me explain. As I stood there crying, the MP's came up the stairs, and one picked me up while the other knocked on the door. It was Mom who opened the door. She was crying when the MP handed me to her. They calmed every one down and told my father that he had to leave for the night. I remember that I felt relief when it was just my mom and me left in the apartment. She was putting the groceries away as she started dinner for us. As I ate my dinner my mom laid on the couch rubbing her stomach and crying.

Before I had finished my plate, there was a knock at the door, and my mom got up to answer it.

4

He said something through the door in German, so mom put on her coat and was helping me with mine as we left the house with the man. He was a taxi driver and he drove us to the hospital. I remember it was dark when we got there. Mom paid him and he drove off. She grabbed me by the hand and headed for the door telling me to hurry up. Of course, I had no idea what was happening or what the hurry was. When we reached the stairs, my mom fell and hit the ground hard. She wasn't moving and I began to scream and cry, but still she didn't get up. I was still screaming when a woman picked me up, and two men picked up my mom and put her on a hospital gurney and pushed her away. I know that something else died in me that night, but I'm just glad I don't remember exactly what it was. I cried myself to sleep, and when I woke up the nurses took me to see my baby sister. Born on March 25, 1968. So, there you have it, the story of my earliest memory.

I was glad to have a sister, and I was glad that my mom did not die. I was, however, not happy that my father was back at the apartment taking care of me until my mom could come home. You see, in my eyes, all of what had happened had made me afraid. Mostly of my father!

I'm glad that I don't remember much of what happened for the next two years. Sure, there are a few little things, like more trips to the grocery store. I remember snow, lots of snow. I remember sledding down the hill on my toboggan. I remember learning to speak German while playing with the kids outside, but that's about all.

CHAPTER 2: INNOCENCE LOST FOREVER

The next memory of merit was when I was six years-old. Mom, Sister, and I had long since left Germany. We lived in Las Vegas, Nevada. North Las Vegas to be precise.

I was in school, Sister in day care, and mom was a secretary. I remember playing in the street on my bike. I remember eating lots of peanut butter and jelly sandwiches. I remember the night our cat got run over in the street. This was my first experience with death. I remember our car caught on fire while we were in it. I remember watching my mom get ready for work. She always played the radio loud and would sing along with it as it played the different songs. I remember that everywhere I went, my sister had to go to. I did my best to look out for her, especially when mom didn't feel well.

You get the picture I'm sure, normal childhood stuff, right? Wrong!!!
The real story begins on the day I was walking home from school. As I got close to my house, I saw a yellow car in the driveway that I had never seen before. And my mom's car was there, too. All of this was wrong and I knew it. Mom was supposed to be at work, and what was up with that yellow car? As I got close to the door it all came rushing back. Fear, anxiety, and for the first time, anger! It was my father, and he was yelling and screaming at my mom. I stood there and listened for just a moment. That's when my mom yelled she was calling the cops. At that moment I opened the door and saw my father

pick up the phone and hit my mom in the head with it. She fell to the floor and my father grabbed her hair and dragged her down the hall to the bedroom. I ran after them screaming for him to let her go. I even grabbed him and tried to pull him off. He turned and hit me, and I flew across the room into the wall. For the first time in my life, I hated!

I ran outside, then down the street, through my friend's back yard and out into the desert. I wiped the blood off of my face with my shirt, and I sat and cried for what seemed like hours. Then, I heard people yelling my name, but not people I recognized. It was the police looking for me. There I was, six years-old, hungry, my face hurt bad, I'd been crying for God knows how long, and the cops were looking for me.

I did what any kid would do, I hid! And I stayed hidden until dark. Then I snuck into a neighbor's camper that sat in his driveway, except when he went hunting. I was glad to see he kept plenty of food in the cupboards, and it had a tv, a bed, a toilet, and an electric cord coming in from the garage. I was set! I stayed in that camper for six days. Then, I had to go out to find something to eat. I walked about five blocks to a grocery store. I filled all my pockets with food and ran out, only to get caught by an off-duty policeman who saw me stealing the food. He knew who I was, of course, since all the police in Vegas were looking for me. He made me give the store the food back, explaining to the manager what had happened to me a week earlier. Then, he put me in his car and drove me home. I was glad to see that my father wasn't there. But I knew my mom, and she was not going to be happy.

I was on restriction after that fiasco, but life went on and things calmed down for a while.

CHAPTER 3: ABANDONED

My next memory is of the event that changed my life forever! As my life got back to normal, such as that was, I noticed that my mom became more and more difficult, for lack of a better word. But I didn't know what was wrong and I was powerless to do anything about it. Then, on the last day of school, I turned the corner and there was that yellow car again. As I walked up the street, all of the things I'd learned from him came rushing back. I'm sure that I was in shock at the time. Why else would I continue walking toward the car?

No screaming, no yelling. Just my father sitting there waiting for me. He told me that Sister and I were coming to live with him. He picked up my sister and opened the door. I followed, but I can't say how I felt. We drove across town to his house and he showed us to our rooms. The closets had all new clothes in them, along with lots of new toys.

All I wanted to know was where my mom was. My father said that we would be going to see her in a couple of months. A couple months! What does a six-year-old know about months? But time went by, and the day came.

Sister and I went to the airport and got on a plane. When the plane landed there was Mom to pick us up. She hugged us both and kissed us at least a hundred times. We drove to her house and met her new husband. She tried to explain why she had left us and why we had to live with our father. To this day, all I remember her saying was, "Blah blah blah!"

What does a seven-year-old know about divorce and custody, and a judge's decision?

The two weeks we spent there flew by, and again we went to the airport. Only this time it was to go home. I call it that because I don't have another word to use. All I know is when that plane door closed, it would be nine years before I would see my mother again. That day, I learned what abandonment was. I wonder what died inside of me that day?

CHAPTER 4: NEW MOMMY #1

I had no way of knowing it would be nine years before I would see Mom again, but I figured out soon enough it would be a long while. My first clue was waiting at the airport with my father when our plane landed. My father said, "Hey guys, this is Gerry. She is your new mom. Come say hello."

I remember grabbing Sister's hand and giving her a little tug. As we walked toward Gerry, she knelt down on one knee and wrapped her arms around us. I let her hug me, and she had a nice warm smile. I'm sure that I went into shock again, because she and my father were just talking away. All I heard was, "Blah blah blah!!!!

Now to sit here and tell you about all of this is hard, mostly because I was only seven years-old at the time, and Sister was just four years-old. I am not sure how long a child can stay in shock. For the next few months or so I don't remember much, and I can't tell you how I felt inside. What I can say for certain is that Gerry was a nice lady. She cared for us and took time to play games with us. She really liked Sister. They would play dress up. Clothes, and make up, and then the modeling show followed. I'm sure it was easier for Gerry to spend all that time with sister because she was younger and didn't remember all the things that I did.

The following is not a memory. I was told this part by Gerry several years later. Apparently, I had had some trouble adjusting after my mom left. Gerry said that I was rebellious and it was hard for her to get near me emotionally. She said that I went out of my way to get into trouble. Which, of course, would piss off old dad and he would spank me. This, of course, made Gerry mad because she didn't think the things I did wrong warranted being hit with a belt. Now I can't say what I even did that was wrong. I just don't remember any of it except for the straw that broke the camel's back.

Back to what I remember. It was Thanksgiving, and we were off to have dinner at my grandmother's house. Sister and I called her "GiGi." She was my mother's mother. And all of my mom's brothers and her sister were there. They were a loud bunch, everyone full of laughter, and making jokes that I didn't understand. Cocktails were always served at GiGi's house. Jack Daniels on the rocks or a cold beer seemed the choice of all involved. Sister and I shared a Dr. Pepper, but we called it our cocktail. Yes, it was strange to be there with all my mom's family, but no Mom! As I write this and try to remember the details, I have no recollection of anyone ever mentioning my mom.

In a house full of half-lit adults, there is not much for a kid to do or say to be part of the occasion. We were to be seen but not heard. So, when Aunt Susie was going to make a quick run to the store, I asked if I could go with her. Susie said I could if it was ok with my father. I went to ask permission and the answer was, "No." But I really wanted to go and I was sure no one would even miss me. So, I did what any kid would do, I lied!
I ran out to the car and jumped in telling Susie nothing about my lie. When we got to the store we

got our items and put them in basket that I was pushing to help out. After paying, Susie bought me an ice cream cone for helping her do the shopping. I sat in the car and ate it, careful not to get it anywhere but in my mouth.

We arrived back at GiGi's house a few minutes later and I was met at the door by my father. He grabbed me and pulled me down the hall and into Uncle Cocoa's room. He told me to drop my pants and turn around. Screaming something about learning to mind him, he pulled off his belt and commenced to whipping the hell out me. He was so mad that he didn't even care where the belt hit me. I was screaming bloody murder with every lash I took. By the time he was to twenty-something lashes I was screaming for him stop, and so was GiGi in the hall just outside of the door. He finally stopped hitting me when I lost control of myself and peed my underpants and all over Cocoa's bed.

It's hard to say what happened next. I remember that there was a lot of commotion with the grown-ups in the other room. GiGi took me into her bathroom and was trying to clean me up, and stop me from crying. When we came out the bathroom everyone was upset, and I use that word loosely. I don't remember how long we stayed or if we ate dinner. The next thing that is clear to me is we were back at home and Gerry was trying to give me first aid were the belt had hit me. She asked me to go to bed early and after the day I had, I agreed. The last thing I heard was her yelling at father about the 26 bleeding welts I had on my back and legs. Finally, I fell asleep!

There is only one more point of this chapter left to tell, but I'm not really sure how to tell you. You see, at some point during the night, after I fell asleep, Gerry and my father argued and my father lost the fight. Gerry had packed her clothes and left, right after she told him she was going to divorce him. At least that's how she explained it to me several years later. As for me, the bruises on the outside healed just fine. But, yes, something more died inside of me that day.

CHAPTER 5: MEMORIES

Up to this point in my story, it's been pretty straight forward about what to tell you. The things I have shared were literally beaten into my subconscious. I've been told that it's unusual for anyone to remember that far into their childhood. If my childhood had been anything other than unusual I might agree. To this day, if I close my eyes, I can see it all happen again just as I told you.

What had died inside of me by the age of eight, was now so large that I could stand on it. The anger and hate that I kept to myself burned so hot that I never got cold.

It's at this point that it will become really hard to determine what is relevant to my story and what is just normal growing up. You see at age eight my memory is much fuller.

I have a million stories that I could tell you, some good and some bad. It has to be human nature or maybe it's my current frame of mind. But as I sit and try to decide what to share with you, it is the bad that I remember most. Why is that?

CHAPTER 6: A BRUTAL CHILDHOOD

After some deliberation I have answered my own question. I just didn't have a very pleasant childhood! That's all there is to it.

Of course, it wasn't always a nightmare. Much of it was just the normal pains of growing up. Except in my case, I always knew what was coming if I screwed up.

Now it was just the three of us: Sister, me, and our father. I suppose I should include the babysitters, even though I don't remember their names. But you see, my father worked in the casinos, and he worked swing shift which was 3-11 pm. Every day I came home just as my father was leaving for work, and I would be in bed by the time he got home. This made my life a little more tolerable. The lack of real supervision only made it that much easier to get in trouble, which I was really good at.

As time passed, I would manage at least one or two spankings a week. This went on for quite some time. Most of my crimes were those of any normal child, except a couple that stick out in my mind. One of those times was when I broke into an empty house that was across the street from ours. I had gone in and vandalized the place pretty good, and for no reason I can remember other than pure meanness. My two friends and I just didn't have anything better to do. I don't even know how we got caught. What I do know is, I couldn't sit down for a week.

This next story is kind of embarrassing, but it is one that stands out in my mind as important.

Something definitely changed in me because of it. As I remember, the neighbor lady had asked me to clean out her garage after her husband had died. She had a dumpster put in the driveway and we agreed on $100 dollars to throw away everything in there. If I saw something I wanted, it was mine to keep. She didn't want any of the stuff in there. I went to work filling the dumpster.

As you can imagine, there was a lot of junk, but I did find a few things worth keeping. I found a CO_2 BB gun still in the original box, there were several jars of change which just sweetened the $100 I was being paid. But what I found most interesting of all was the box full of porno magazines. You see, up to this point in life I didn't pay much attention to girls. But as I looked at those magazines just full of naked women doing all sorts of unmentionable things my curiosity began to grow.

As a matter of fact, you might say a pervert was born. I was so intrigued by all of it, that I found myself sneaking off to look at them every time I got a chance. One day I came home and found my whole collection of smut laying on my bed. I'm not sure what was worse, the anticipation of what was coming, or the actual beating itself. It was early the next morning when my father walked into my room. He already had his belt off and he started in with a bunch of questions. I didn't make much effort to answer them because it was obvious that no matter what I said that he planned on whipping me good. After that was over, he told me to stay in my room and think about what I had done wrong.

As I laid on my bed considering what had just happened, all I remember coming up with was this question: Why was it ok for me to have a gun to play with, but looking at naked women was a crime? I can't say that something died in me that day, but something definitely changed!

You should know that I didn't come to understand what it was until much later in life. On that day, I decided that I was going to do everything in my power to make my father's life a living hell. There was just no other way to get back at him than to make him suffer the way he did me.

CHAPTER 7: NEW MOMMY #2

Here we are in my story at about the age of ten-years-old. It was at this time when my father began to date the lady who watched me and Sister after we got out of school each day. Her name was Betty, and she was a nice lady. She had kids of her own that were around the same age as us. Two girls and a boy that were older than me, and a girl that was just younger than sister. All of us kids got along really well for the most part. Going to the babysitter every day was actually fun. Betty always helped us with our homework after school, she had plenty of toys to play with, and she made nice dinners every day. She was an attractive woman and she had a real pleasant way about herself that made you like her without having to give it a lot of effort. It's no wonder that my father took notice and asked her to marry him.

You will have to bear with me as I try to put together in words all that happened over the course of the next few years. There is a lot to tell, and so much of it over laps because I lived in a house full of people. I am listing them for you by order of oldest to youngest. Father, Betty, Peggy, Patti, Bill, myself, Sister, and Rashelle.

Betty was a religious woman. A Mormon to be precise. This alone is a whole can of worms that I will do my best to try to explain as is needed in the story. But I will start by saying that up to this point in my life, Jesus and God were never spoken of unless someone was using their names to swear.

I feel it's important to tell you that to this point in life I was a quiet and timid boy, for reasons I'm sure you have come to on your own. With the arrival of my new step family I was given a little more breathing room. There were a lot of adjustments that had to be made as we tried to put all those people in one three-bedroom house. And with Betty there looking after all us kids, it didn't take long to notice things were going to be way different than what I was used to.

The first big change that I noticed was that the spankings had come to a screeching halt. The second big change was we started going to church every Sunday. The third thing was that I wasn't responsible for every little thing that went wrong. Life was a different thing all together. At least for a while.

The thing I remember that didn't change was my mom was still gone. I also remember that I still was full of anger, even hate, toward my father for all the things he had done to me in the past. It will come as no surprise to you that one day I found some trouble to get into worthy of a good beating. Which my father was happy to give me. But you see, at this point I was a little older, and a lot colder on the inside. When I was getting the spanking, I refused to cry. Which only made my father that much more enraged. So, he kept hitting me and I kept biting my tongue. This made Betty quite angry and she barged into the room to stop my father from hitting me. I left the room but the fight had just begun. When I think back I don't remember what it was I did, and I'm not sure how old I was. What I am sure of is that things began a to fall apart with my father and Betty on that day.

Which brings me to the next major life experience in which something more died inside. Once again, I was in trouble, over what I cannot say. But whatever the case was, I had run away from home. Having been gone for several days, my father had had plenty of time to build up his anger with me. So much so that when he found me walking the streets, he pulled over and chased me. When he finally caught me, he was fit to be tied. He wasted no time with a belt but went straight to hitting me with his hand. Screaming stuff at me the whole time. Now I don't remember what he was screaming, only that he expected an answer. What he got instead was a go to hell look and silence. Which turned out be more effective than I had hoped. He hit me in the throat with the back of his hand. I gasped for air, but it was slow coming. I was having trouble swallowing as my wits slowly came back. I just sat there numb with anger, feeling helpless and beat up. We arrived at juvenile hall and he took me in to the police to teach me a lesson. Running away from home, it turns out, is a crime in Las Vegas. So, in I went and away he went!

Once inside, they began the booking process which included seeing the nurse. She saw the bruise on my neck from when he hit me in the throat. As I told her what had happened she continued to ask me all sorts of questions. I answered her point blank in my anger. When she was done with her report she asked me if wanted to file charges against him. "Can I do that?" I asked. "Yes, you can," she replied. As it turns out, it's a worse crime to beat your children. So, instead of juvenile hall I was put in child welfare housing. I stayed there for about a week. On Sunday it was visiting day. All of us kids went in to watch a movie in the day room. If they called your name you went somewhere else to visit. When they called my name, I didn't answer them. When they called again, I didn't answer. So they stopped the movie and found me in the crowd and pulled me out of the room. The woman that had been looking for me asked why I didn't answer when she called my name? Because I don't want to talk to him, I said. "But don't you want to go home?" she asked. "No! I like it here."

A few minutes later the woman was back. "Will you see your step mother?" she asked? I answered yes, but only her I insisted. When Betty came into the room it was evident even to me that she was frazzled. She hugged me and sat down. She talked softly to me, explaining that me filing charges against my father was causing a lot of problems for him, and in turn, the rest of the family. She explained to me that an investigator was going around asking a lot of questions about my father to people like the bishop of our church, my father's boss where he worked, several of the neighbors, and my teacher at school. Betty then told me if I didn't drop the charges they might take my sister and make her live in in the same place I was. Finally, she said, if the charges are dropped that I could come home and we could put all of this behind us and move on and no punishment would be put on me for whatever it was I did.

I reluctantly agreed to Betty's proposal, only because I didn't want my sister to suffer for my sins. It took a little while, but I was released and we went home. The ride home was a quiet one. No one spoke a single word.

It was much later in life that I came to realize what It was that died in me during this whole ordeal. It was the knowledge that my father would do whatever it took to cover his own ass, regardless of how badly he treated others. And that he had no remorse for the things he had done to me. All that mattered was himself. It's a hard thing to find out that the only reason we had gone to live with him and the reason he had gotten custody of us was to spite my mother. He didn't love me or my sister, he just hated my mother that much. The innocence of youth was just about gone!!!

As always, time continued to pass, and all of us kids got older. I was a teenager now and we all know how hard that can be. At least it was for me.

CHAPTER 8 – THE BEGINNING OF THE END

The tension in the house slowly eased. Everyone went about pretending that nothing was wrong. But it was there, just below the surface, and no one dared to talk about it. "It" being the biggest pink elephant you've ever seen. We were all fooling ourselves, trying to pretend we were a family.

The honeymoon was over. Betty and my father were still married, but the love was gone. The only reason they were still together was the business they had started together had left them both a little financially challenged. The business however was a good excuse to stay gone and my father worked that angle to a tee.

As for the rest of us, we did what we could to try and act like family. With all us kids growing up so fast, it seemed we were always going in a hundred different directions. And that went double for me.

I had a lot of stuff going on as a teenager. There was school, I worked at night and on weekends for Betty, all of us kids had chores we were responsible for, and I was on probation as well. It almost sounds like a normal life. But it was anything but normal, and it will take some doing to explain it all to you. It was like a chain reaction how things played out as I come to the age of fifteen.

You hopefully remember my grandmother, "GiGi." Well, after that scene we had on Thanksgiving, Sister and I never were allowed to go back to her house to visit. And, as a kid, I had no understanding of why. Even to this day, I can only speculate as to what was said between my father and GiGi.

The high school I went to was less than a block away from GiGi's house. Since I was not allowed to go there or even talk about her, it should come as no surprise to you that that is exactly what I did. And, yes, I got in trouble for it! But GiGi was my mother's mother, and I figured that her house was the best place to find out information on my mother's whereabouts.

It's at this same time that I was already on probation for stealing a car. When my father found out that I had been going to GiGi's house he lost it. And, you know that I got the hell beat out of me, AGAIN!

After the beating, my father told me to go to my room and stay there until further notice. Which I promptly ignored. I ran straight out of the house and was gone before anyone knew what happened. I didn't find out until later about all the drama that took place while I was gone. My father hitting me again was apparently a deal breaker for Betty. By deal breaker, I mean Broke! They were fighting so much that no one even bothered to come look for me. Which was a huge mistake on their part.

My plan to make my father's life a living hell was working. And working way better than I had hoped. Betty had told my father she wanted a divorce, and they should do whatever it took to split the business and that he should find somewhere else to live ASAP!

Meanwhile, I had gone to the CircusCircus Casino and stolen some of the really large stuffed animals from the arcade. I sold them to tourists for

$100 each. From there, I went straight to GiGi's house and told her the whole story about my father beating me again because I had come to see her. I told her that I had enough money to buy a bus ticket and that I needed her to give me my mother's address in Kansas. It was at this minute that GiGi got real quiet and a strange look came over her face. I asked her again for the address, but she just looked at me. I raised my voice and insisted she give it to me!

"Sit down!" she said to me sharply. "There is something I have to tell you. Your mother doesn't live in Kansas anymore. She lives right here in Vegas."

I was in shock again! I can't tell you how that made me feel. My mother was living in the same city as me and had not even bothered to come and see me. "Why the hell not?" I thought to myself. My mind was flooded with all kinds of confused thoughts and a wave of emotions came over me so suddenly. I couldn't even recognize all of them. I just sat there and started to cry. GiGi got up and went to her desk. She grabbed a piece of paper and wrote my mother's address on it and handed it to me.

She said, "It was bound to happen, so why not today." She told me to clean up and get going before my father showed up. She had called him the moment I had arrived at her house.

I left in hurry, jumping two fences and running across the Interstate. I made it to the mall, and grabbed a slice of pizza and a pop while I waited on the bus. I was still in shock, I suppose, because I don't remember exactly how I made it to my mom's house. But there I was, standing in front of a small apartment. I'm not sure how long I waited, but she finally came home.

Apparently, GiGi had not called her, because she was really surprised to see me standing there. I was crying as I gave her a big hug. She, of course, started to cry and hugged me back. As we went inside she asked me how I had found her. I told her the story of what had happened in the last couple of days and how I had come to know that she was in Vegas. As we sat and talked, all I wanted to know was why she had not come to see us?

Her answer made my blood boil! As she spoke I felt the last of my childhood innocence die inside of me. I mean to say, it was gone, and I would never recover any of it.

"I didn't think you wanted to see me," she replied. "I have written you letters, sent cards, and sent presents to you. Which I see you got, but never did you answer me, or say thank you." "What presents and letters?" I asked. "I never got any presents nor did I get any letters," I insisted. My mom looked at me and said, "You are wearing a shirt that I sent you for Christmas this year!"

I sat there and told my mother that in almost nine years, I had never seen a letter, a card, or a present with her name on it. And at that moment, I realized what a bastard my father truly was! He had been keeping letters from me all these years and giving me presents, that my mother had sent, rewrapped with his name on them. Did I mention what a bastard he is?

We spent several hours talking about all kinds of things. None of which were very pleasant. It was getting late and mom suggested that she drive me home. She had to work the next day and needed to get some rest.

I told her that it was not a good idea for her to go anywhere near that house. Besides, I had no intentions of going back myself. Ever!

CHAPTER 9: THE END HAS ARRIVED

Here we are at the end of my childhood. I am only a few months from being sixteen-years-old. Because of all the drama in my life at home, and all the time I spent as a runaway or in juvenile hall, I had managed to flunk out of tenth grade. That in itself left me with an empty feeling inside, to say nothing of how it affected my already low self-esteem. I kept so much bottled up in side of me that I was angry all the time. But so much of what was wrong with my life was no fault of my own. I suppose that I was lucky that the court ordered shrink was able to see that and wrote it down that way in his report.

I was back in court for violating the terms of my probation. The judge presiding over my case was intent on finding out why I insisted on getting in trouble so much. She had me standing in front of her bench asking me if I wanted to go to a juvenile work camp. Which is basically prison, only for kids. I said my piece, and when I was finished she told me to take a seat.

She asked Betty what her thoughts were. Betty said her piece and when she finished the judge thanked her and said she could be seated.

The judge asked my father to stand. When he stood up, instead of asking him questions like she had done with Betty and me, she laid into him like no one had ever done before. I mean she gave him the first, second, and third-degree ass-chewing.

It was all I could do to not break out laughing at him. The big bully, my father, had to stand there and just take it. When she was done giving him the what for, she announced that we would take a recess for lunch while she made her decision.

That was a long hour, and as she sat down, I was thinking that my goose was probably cooked. When she began to speak, I couldn't believe my ears. While we were at lunch my other grandmother had called the judge from Oklahoma. All us kids called her, "O'ma."

O'ma had convinced the judge not to send me to prison, but instead, I would be going to spend the summer with her. While I was there, I would be working for my uncle in his construction company. But mostly I would be in a stress-free environment. I would also be getting regular meals, regular sleep, regular work hours and pay, and there would be no beatings. I would have the whole summer to get my act together before school started the next fall.

As the judge finished explaining to me what she hoped I would do with this chance she was giving me, she also reminded me that I was going to turn sixteen that summer. Which meant that I would no longer be a child in the eyes of the courts since sixteen is the legal age to be charged for any crime as an adult in Nevada.

She looked me straight in the eye and said, "It's all up to you what happens from now on, do you understand what I'm telling you?" I nodded my head, because I was too shocked to speak! She hit the block with her hammer and said, "Court is adjourned."

So, there you have it! That is how my childhood ended. But that's not all of the story. There are a few other things you need to know before I move on.

This is where we come to the proverbial fork in the road. Not just for me, but everyone involved. My father and Betty were now separated waiting on the divorce to be final. Which will come to pass while I'm gone for the summer.

My mother had filed custody papers to get my sister away from my father. Which gave me a sense of relief. Even more so when my father agreed to the terms without a fight. Sister had just turned twelve in March, and I was glad she would not have to go through her teen years in fear of my father. You see, my mother had just married her third husband, and he seemed to be a really good man.

As for me, it was as if the weight of the world was lifted off my shoulders. Uncle Ronnie would be there to get me in just a couple of days.

CHAPTER 10: A CHANGE OF SCENERY

There is a lot to be said for a change of scenery. I can't tell you how much I enjoyed being away from Las Vegas, or maybe I should say, the drama of life in Las Vegas. Oklahoma was another world to me, and as I sit here telling this story, I can only remember good things about that summer.

Living with O'ma was a real pleasure. She was a simple woman, who took great pleasure in the life that she had made for herself. She was old enough to be retired, yet still young enough to do whatever she took a notion to do. And, at this present time, she was set on helping me try to get my head on straight.

Every morning she would rise early to go out and water her garden. Then, she would wake me up and head to kitchen to make us both breakfast. I would hit the kitchen dressed for work and we would eat our eggs and bacon. I always washed them down with chocolate milk. After we did the dishes she would drive me to Ronnie's house. It was only five blocks, but she insisted on driving me.

Ronnie was always up when I arrived in the morning. He would tell me to start loading the tools in the truck, and he was patient to teach me the names of all tools. When the other guys showed up, we hit the supply house and then on to the job or jobs, whatever the case was. When our work was done it was back to Ronnie's house. All the guys sat around drinking beer while I learned how to maintain the tools.

He would talk to me about all kinds of things while I was learning the things he thought a growing boy should know. One of our discussions was about what kind of car did I want to drive home in.

I told him I had no idea what I wanted. I told him about my stealing a car back home in Vegas, and I told him that my father had made it pretty clear that I was not going to be getting a license or a car until I left home. Ronnie just laughed, then he looked at me and said, "It's a good thing you left early!" Still laughing, he asked me if my father happened to tell me about the several cars that my father and his buddies stole when they were kids? I shook my head no, but Ronnie smiled at me and said, "I'll tell you about it sometime.

When work was finished, he would take me back to O'ma's house. I would go around back and come in through the laundry room. O'ma had my house coat hung over the door, so I stripped right there and went straight to the shower. When I emerged all clean and shiny we would sit down at the table and have our dinner.

After dinner we would sit and talk, or watch a show on tv, but my favorite thing was beating her at dominoes. And so it went that this was my new life.

After only a couple of weeks, it seemed that everyone was adjusted to my being there, and that went double for me. Until the Saturday morning that Ronnie showed up at O'mas house with a newspaper in his hand. "Get dressed," he said, "I've found you a car". We all piled into his van and away we went.

It was a 1957 Chevy, it barely ran and the inside looked like a dog had chewed on it for his dinner. The body being straight was its only redeeming feature. We made the deal with the car's owner and he handed me the title and an extra set of keys. Ronnie told me to stay close behind him as we made our way back to his house. I pulled my car into the driveway and shut it off. Ronnie opened the hood and told me that I was going to have to rebuild that engine.

I just stood there like a deer in the headlights. Ronnie cracked open a beer and started telling me to unhook this, and disconnect that, and don't forget to drain the oil before I started. I just looked at him and said, "What's a carburetor and how do you drain the oil?" You see, I knew nothing about working on a car, and the only thing I knew about tools was what I had learned in the last couple of weeks.

It was slow going at first, but I caught on. Step by step, I learned the ins and outs of auto repairs. It was lucky for me that I had the whole summer to learn. Ronnie would supervise, I did the work, and O'ma was my chauffeur when I needed to hunt parts. This was how I spent the summer: I worked all day on the job, and all my evenings and weekends on the car.

Before I knew it my sixteenth birthday had arrived. It was quite a party that O'ma put together. We all went out to dinner together, then back to her house for pie and coffee. They all sang happy birthday to me and then I opened presents. Now as I tell of this festive occasion, it has occurred to me that this is the first birthday that I have any recollection of to this point in life. That is sad to me and I'm glad that I did not realize it until now.

My summer was just about over, and the car was almost complete. The three of us would have a lot to talk about in the next couple weeks. As the summer came to an end, my plan for the future become clear to me as well. I was going to finish high school, and graduate on time with my classmates even if it killed me!

As I finish this chapter, I think it's important to tell you that nothing died inside of me that summer. If anything, I think that I may have actually lived for the first time in my life. I know it seemed that way at the time!

CHAPTER 11: ON MY OWN

As I returned to Vegas in my 1957 Chevy, it became clear to me that everyone was now on the paths that they had chosen. My father's divorce from Betty was finally complete. My mother was married to her new husband, and they had custody of my sister. And, I was 16 and on my own. I had made arrangements with Betty to rent a room from her and to work for her as a means to support myself. Living with her made it easy for me to go to school with the few friends that I had.

I will not bore you with the details of the next two years, except to say that I was living a full life. I was able to achieve my goal of graduating high school on time, with my class! I was also free to go and visit anyone I chose to, such as GiGi, my mother, and my sister. I also had several girl friends that I spent time with, but these relationships were of a casual nature. It seemed that my biggest problem was listening to everyone trying to give me advice, which I found humorous because the people giving the advice did nothing but contradict one another. It's hard to take advice from people who can barely run their own lives, if you know what I mean?

Now I suppose it's important to tell you that even though I was able to do whatever it was that I wanted, it was by no means a picnic being 16 or 17-years-old and on my own. I had so much that I was responsible for that play time was scarce. But then, anything was better than being abused!
Which brings us to the next pivot point in my life.

I just graduated from high school and I had no idea what to do with my life. You see, all my plans for life had only been planned through this day. I had not considered the fact that I would actually get this far. So now I was faced with what to do next!

All my thoughts kept bringing me back to the summer I had spent working for my uncle in Oklahoma. How I had felt so good and peaceful during that time away from all the drama that was my life in those days. So, I packed up all my belongings in a glad trash bag and away I went. At this time in life it seemed this was my best option, but knowing what I know now, I wish like hell that I had had another option to consider. If only life came with an instruction manual!

CHAPTER 12: YOU CAN NEVER GO BACK

Here I am, not quite 18 years-old, and back in Oklahoma. I was staying with O'ma and I had gone back to work with Ronnie, but he didn't have enough work to keep me busy full time. Ronnie was also dealing with a nasty divorce of his third wife. This meant that I didn't spend much time at his house like I had done before. He was drinking a lot, and using drugs on top of that. I just did my job, and then home to O'mas I would go.

Around Christmas time, I took a part time job at the mall selling men's clothes. This was where I met a girl named Misty. She was a very sexy blonde, about 5' 7" tall and weighed about 110 lbs. She was very outgoing and very fashionable to boot. Why she decided on me to be her boyfriend is a mystery to me still. We went steady for the next couple of years. During this time, my life was about as normal as one could hope for and in my case more normal than it had ever been.

As I approached the age of 20, I wanted to move out of O'mas house and get my own place. But I wasn't making enough money with Ronnie because work was so inconsistent. There was just no way of knowing if I would make enough to pay my bills each month.

I went out and found a job working in a bingo hall. Finding this job was, in fact, a day I shall never forget. I had showed up to my interview on time, and dressed in a very nice outfit. The manager, Steve, sat down and looked at my application and then then looked at me. He looked me straight in the eye and asked, "Do you drink or use drugs?" I was a little shocked by his question, but I told him that I did not! As he stood to shake my hand, he said, "That will change! Get yourself a good pair of running shoes and be here tomorrow at 10:30am."

As I left the bingo hall, I was feeling pretty good about myself. I was ready to move forward with all the things I had been planning for my future.

But as I tell you this story so many years later, I wish that I had never gone to work the next day. God only knows how different my life might have been! And nothing I remember died in me on that day. It was, however, the first step down a long winding path that almost cost me my life. But let's not get ahead of ourselves.

As I continued working at my new career as a bingo caller, my relationship with Misty began to fall apart. She was not happy with the hours I was working, and she did not like it that I had started closing the bars every night after work. But it was when she found out that I was using cocaine that she decided to dump me.

I was crushed at first, because Misty and I had so many plans for the future together and now she refused to even talk to me. It is the irony of the whole situation that left me feeling like I had just wasted two years of my life. The job that had allowed me to make enough money to get married and support us was the same job that split us up. And a little more died inside of me because of the break up with Misty!

When you're 20-years-old, making ridiculous amounts of money, drinking and drugging, and living a life of non-stop partying, it doesn't take long to realize that best way to get over a girl is to get under a new one. So, I went to work!

You see, all my life I was so beaten down that I was what you might call a social misfit. But something about that cocaine had changed me. I was becoming a flaming extrovert. Or in simpler terms, the life of the party!

This was all my life had become, one party over and waiting for the next to begin. I woke up every day sometime after noon, took a shower, got dressed, met my friends for dinner, and off to work we would go. We would all get high just before work began at 5:00, then after work we bought a 12 pack of beer and would kill it on the way to the club. Then, we did a bump of cocaine before we went in and started drinking. The goal for each night was to find a girl to have sex with once the bar closed. And that was all life was about - making enough money to stay drunk and high, and staying drunk and high to deal with the game of the one-night stands. And I was really good at playing the game. So much so, that we used to bet $100 dollars each to see who could go the most nights in a row with a different girl each night, without repeating with a girl you had already slept with during the bet. If you missed a night, you lost your money. The last man standing won the pot.

Now I know what you're thinking, and you're right. I was nothing more than a male whore! But I told myself that I liked it, but maybe it was the cocaine talking! All I know is that I liked being popular, as well as being the life of the party. So, this continued on for years. Even when I got busted for possession of cocaine, it did nothing to slow me down since I only went on probation!

EMPTY!! That's how I felt at any given moment. ADDICTED!! That's all my life was about. I was addicted to money, power, sex, drugs, alcohol, and popularity. I was literally consumed by addiction in an effort to take the empty feeling away. Although none of it took away how I felt inside, I was still willing to keep giving it a chance to work. I think that is the definition of insanity, if I'm not mistaken!

And insanity is definitely the right word to describe my life!

Now as we move on with the story, you should know that I am sparing you all the gory details about my sin and debauchery. Even though there are those who might want to hear the absolute truth about the debauchery, I will spare you!

CHAPTER 13: A CHILD IS BORN

The next big life altering event was the birth of my daughter, when I was about twenty-three years-old. I had left Oklahoma and was now living in San Diego, California with my baby's momma. Darla was her name and my daughter's name was Bryonna.

Darla and I had gone to California to get away from dope game, and we managed to stay clean the whole time that Darla was pregnant. But now that Bryonna was born there was nothing keeping us from getting high. Now I should just say, nothing to keep me from getting high. But every time I turned around, I was trying to either get Darla high so she would have sex with me or I was trying to cut her off so she would leave me alone. Ours became a love-hate relationship that neither of us wanted to continue being part of.

I told her that regardless of hers and my situation, I wanted to be part of Bryonna's life. Darla promised me that I could do that with no argument from her. We did our best to be civil to each other for Bryonna's sake. Darla was a good mother and she did a great job of raising Bryonna. I saw Bryonna as often as I could, and I always made sure she had all the things a little girl needed, which was me sending money for whatever lessons she was taking at the time, or just for things like school clothes. The most important thing to me was that she was a happy child and that she knew that she was loved.

Up to now in this story I have told you everything that was happening in chronological order.

But because of the difficulty I am having telling you about Bryonna, I think that I should just finish telling you about her.

There really is not much left to say, but what is left hurts me so bad that I can't stop crying while writing this. You see, she only lived to be 11 years-old. She was spending the night with her friends at a sleep over, as kids love to do. While they slept, a space heater caught fire in the hallway just outside the room they were sleeping in. The house went up in flames and all three girls burned to death in the fire.

Goodbye, Bryonna. I guess that heaven needed you back!

As I sit here with tears rolling down my face, I am having trouble finding words to tell you what died in me on that day, but I am sure that you will understand if I just don't try to find them.

CHAPTER 14: NO MATTER WHERE YOU GO, THERE YOU ARE

I'm sorry about that last chapter. I just didn't know how else to tell you.

Let's back up a little bit to when I am about 26-years-old. Darla and I were done as a couple and she had gone home to Oklahoma. I chose to go back to Vegas, and I brought my new girlfriend there with me. Her name was Renee and she was there with me only because of all the drugs that I had at my disposal. I kept her there because she was absolutely beautiful and she was bisexual. Being with her had taken my partying to a whole new level! But strangely enough, it had taken my emptiness to a whole new level as well. It was during my time with her that I managed to lose my whole sense of self-worth. My addictions where who I was! No matter what I did or where I ran to, I was always there. I just couldn't hide from that man in the mirror.

I could go on for hours telling you about all the gory details of our escapades, but that would only boil down to what I am about to tell you, because it is the whole point of even bringing Renee into the story. You see, once again, my relationship was coming to an end, but I was too messed up to even see it.

In my drug induced state of mind, I had come to the conclusion that the only way I was going to hang on to Renee was to ask her to marry me. I got off of work early one day and drove to the mall. I went in to a jewelry store and bought a ring. Then, I drove home to get Renee and take her out to dinner and propose to her with the ring that I had just purchased.

Boy, was I surprised when I walked through the bedroom door. Or, should I say, they were surprised when I walked through the bedroom door? Either way, it was quite a scene. Renee was having sex with my best friend. His name was Steve and he jumped up when he saw me standing there. Renee also jumped up and said, "Let me explain!"

There was nothing that I wanted to hear from her, so I shoved her by the face until the back of her head cracked against the wall. This, of course, took the wind right out of her sails, and she fell across the bed. Steve, who was standing beside the bed naked, decided that he was going to defend Renee's honor. He lunged at me and took a swing. He missed hitting me, but I did not miss when I swung back. When my fist connected with his nose it made the most horrible sound and blood went everywhere. I had knocked him out and broke his nose with just one punch.

At this point, the adrenaline was pumping through me like rocket fuel. I went into such a rage that, I swear to you, I was spinning and screaming at the top of my lungs every cuss word that I knew. I picked up the tv and threw it right through the front window of the apartment, followed closely by Steve and Renee's clothes. By the time I was done spinning, the apartment was almost empty. I sat down in my recliner and tried to calm myself.

I heard a knock at the door. It was the police, and guess what, I was under arrest. That lady cop had her gun out and was pointing it straight at my head. Her partner took me outside and handcuffed me to the stairs.

It wasn't long before an ambulance arrived and took Steve and Renee to the hospital. As the ambulance left, the police put me in their car and carted me off to jail!

I was released 30 days later. I went to Sister's house and gathered up my things that she and her husband had gone and packed for me while I was locked up. I said my goodbyes and drove into the sunrise.

I would like to tell you that something died in me because of this event, but that would be a lie. The truth is, there was nothing left inside of me to kill. I was completely void and empty inside. In fact, if i had just killed myself then, I would have done the world a great service. I wasn't worth the bullet it would take to kill me!!

CHAPTER 15 – THE SEARCH FOR ME BEGINS

As you have probably guessed, I returned to Oklahoma. I was physically tired and morally bankrupt as I tried to pick up the pieces of my life and start over once again. But I was like a dog returning to eat his vomit. In 29 years of life, I had learned nothing and was a slave to my addictions. I was about to learn a valuable lesson and not a moment too soon.

I was working in a bingo hall again, which was where I met Linda. She was an OK looking girl, not nearly as pretty as my past girlfriends, but she had a way about her that I found appealing. She and I would just get together and go out. It was what you might call a casual friendship with benefits, and the benefits weren't all of a sexual nature. She was a good listener and I believe she genuinely cared for me. After we had been seeing each other for a while she had heard all she needed hear.

You see, we had gone out one night and had drinks and done a little too much coke. Nothing out of the ordinary, except that I had gotten real emotional and was crying about my life as a child. How I got beat all the time, and how mean my father was to me, and so on and so forth. Blah blah blah!

Linda looked at me and asked, "How old are you?"

"Thirty tomorrow," I replied.

"And when did you leave home?" she asked.

"When I was 16," I replied.

Then she looked at me, straight in the eyes and said, "Do you realize that you have been beating yourself up almost as long as he did!"

And it was as if someone had just turned on the lights in a pitch-black room. The light was a good thing, but it was hard to look at after being in the dark for so long.

Linda must have seen that I was struggling with what she had just dropped on me. So, she picked up my phone and dialed my father's number. She handed the phone to me and said, "When he answers, just tell him that you forgive him, and hang up."

That's just what I did! And if you can believe it, I felt better immediately. Linda then told me just to let it all go. She said, "You're a big guy, and I doubt you would let anyone beat you up without a fight, so stop beating yourself up."

I left Linda's house the next morning, which just happened to be my 30th birthday. When I got home I sat down and thought about what had happened the night before. I enjoyed the freedom I felt from the chains having been removed from my soul. And in that moment of time I realized that I was still in there somewhere and needed to be found. I made up mind to go looking for me. Not the me that was walking around that others saw and talked to, but the me that lived inside of that body. I knew right where to look. I made up my mind to say "no" to the addictions that were keeping me from myself. I quit selling and using dope first, then I quit drinking and going to bars. Amazing as it may sound the rest just seemed to disappear. I found myself right where I knew I was, buried under a pile of vices.

The light was on, and it got easier to see as time went by. I had found myself again, but it would take a little while to fully recover from the abuse that I had done to myself.

CHAPTER 16: THE ROAD TO HELL IS PAVED WITH GOOD INTENTIONS

As we move forward with the story there is still much that I need to tell you. I will start by saying that it was a good thing that I was able to step away from all of my addictions. It was easier to quit, than it was to deal with the effects of quitting.

My body and mind had been so polluted for so long that quitting came as a real shock to my system. I was having the most unbelievable nightmares. In them, I was being chased by faceless beings who wanted to kill me. The worst ones were when I dreamed that I was getting high and I would wake up soaking wet and totally panic stricken. It sometimes took hours to go back to sleep, and even when I did fall asleep again, it was nothing for me to start in with those dreams again.

I managed to stay clean for a whole year, but being clean really wasn't what I hoped it would be. It was nice to not be angry all the time, but I missed being numb! I also missed the money! Being poor sucked, really bad!

So, I gave up the fight. It was just so much easier to join in than to stick to my guns. Now I know what you're thinking, but it's actually worse than what you think it is. You see, cocaine and Ecstasy were no longer the drugs of choice. Crystal methamphetamine was now all the rave! Anyone who was anyone was high on meth. I went to see my old friends and got back in the game.

I managed to keep it under control as far as using was concerned, but selling was a whole other story. It was an epidemic on the streets. People just kept coming! I was making incredible money, but having a hell of time with the traffic.

I knew I was getting hot on the police radar, because so many people I knew were getting busted. When my mom called and offered me a place to live if I would go back to school and obtain a degree in culinary arts, it was not that hard of a decision to make. Once again, I packed my stuff in a Glad trash bag and drove into the sunset.

It wasn't until a couple of years later that I found out that I had left town on the same day that my connection had got run in on by the cops. They even asked about my whereabouts, but I had told no one that I was leaving. I had literally missed getting busted by just a couple of hours. How lucky could I get?

At age 34, I was on my way back to school, which had always been a dream of mine. Finish school and travel the world working on a cruise ship! It seemed to me that finally things would be better.

CHAPTER 17: CALIFORNIA DREAMING

I was back in San Diego, AGAIN! But I was away from the dope again as well. My mom and her husband, Mike, seemed glad that I chose to take them up on their offer. To be honest, I was glad that I had chosen it as well, although it was not a hard decision to make. I had always been pretty good in the kitchen, so going to culinary school was really exciting.

I am not going to say much about culinary school, except that it was absolutely awesome! I loved every minute of it! To this day I still consider it to be one of the best experiences of my life.

Too soon school was over, and it was time to move out of Mom's house and get my own place. Instead of getting a place by myself, I decided to move in with a girl I had been dating while I was in school. I only did this because I wasn't making very much money working as a chef. I didn't really even like Michelle that much. She was just a girl I was using for sex and a place to live until I found a better deal.

Yeah, I know what you're thinking, and you're right to think it! And looking back now as I'm telling you what I did, I can honestly say that I wish I hadn't done it. You've heard the phrase, "Hell has no fury like a woman scorned!" Well, let me tell you, that is an understatement.

When she got wind that I was looking to move out of her place, she went ballistic. I was asleep on the couch when she decided to go snooping through my wallet and phone, which was where I had put the list of numbers to call about places for rent. She jumped on top of me and hit me in the mouth, giving me a bloody lip. Then, she hit me in the eye and her ring cut my face open. The whole time she was screaming what a SOB that I was. I tried to push her off of me, but she wouldn't let go. I just stood up and tried to leave, but she still had hold of me. I screamed at her to let go, but she had no intentions of doing so. After giving her one more chance to comply, I'd had enough. I hit her one time on the side of her head and she went limp. As soon as I saw what I had done, I ran from the house and went straight to phone and called the cops.

Finally, the police had issued a warrant for my arrest. I turned myself in and waited for my day in court. The judge listened to what I had to say, and since she hadn't bothered to come to court herself, he no choice but to rule in my favor. A ruling that came with a warning. If he ever saw me in his court room again, I was going to prison. No passing Go and no collecting 200 dollars!!!

There you have it, I had dodged a bullet again. But I knew Michelle would never leave me alone. Once again, I drove into the proverbial sunset heading for Oklahoma.

CHAPTER 18: OUT OF THE FRYING PAN AND INTO THE FIRE

At this point in my story, it might be a good idea to get up and get yourself something to drink and maybe use the restroom. Things from here on out get pretty real. That is to say that I am about to learn some lessons that I wish I would have never had the occasion to learn. I think it's only fair to warn you that it's going to be as hard for you to read as it is for me to write!

Arriving in Oklahoma again brought back a flood of bad feelings. I felt like I was running out of options, and it was as if I was trapped in a maze that had no way out.

Oklahoma City is a pretty big place, but in reality it like a small town. No matter how much you try to stay out of sight, eventually you will run into someone you know. Which was exactly what happened to me! I'm sure you have already guessed that I was about to be back in the dope game!

It all started with me just selling to a small group of people so I could do mine for free. But the meth epidemic on the streets of Oklahoma City was worse than when I had left a couple of years ago, and my connection had the best dope available on the streets. It wasn't long before I was selling several ounces a day, which was making for me a nice chunk of change. I also had a job working as a crew chief on a drywall crew that paid pretty well.

It wasn't long before I was right in my comfort zone. The days went by, one after the other, and nothing much changed, except every once in while someone would get it in their head to rob me. I won't go into detail about these robberies except to tell you that it happened several times over the next few years. I've been pistol whipped, beaten, shot, stabbed, and run over. Some of these things more than once, but that's just part of the game and you get used to it.

I continued on like this for a little over a year. All I did was work and party. I didn't bother with looking for a girlfriend because there was always some strung out girl willing to do anything just to get high. I had all my bases covered and could do no wrong. I was in control of everything, or so I thought.

One day, O'ma came to my house to deliver a message from my sister's husband. My sister had passed away and the funeral was less than two days away. Derek wanted me to know and he hoped I would be there for the funeral.

I have not shared a lot about my sister in this story, but I will tell you now, Sister and I were always close. No matter what I did, meaning all the things I have told you and a bunch more that I didn't, she never once turned her back on me. She always loved me and I loved her. Her death came as quite a blow to me, but I assured Derek that I would be there.

After my call was finished, I thanked O'ma for bringing me the message and walked her to her car. As she drove off, I had a sinking feeling in my stomach, but I told myself it was just the news about Sister that had me upset.

I went back inside to collect myself and to get high. I mean I got blasted! I grabbed a huge shard of meth and crushed it on a mirror. Then I got a piece of glass tubing and a torch and I heated the tube until it was almost about to melt. I put the other end to my nose and sucked up about 2 grams of dope. What went into the hot end vaporized instantly and turned into smoke by the time it hit my nose on the cool end. I felt the meth run through me as I opened my mouth to exhale. As I fell back on the couch from the rush, I began to cry like I never had before in my entire life. This went on for the next 24 hours while I packed and cleaned house, so I could leave town and not worry about what any would be burglars would try to steal.

By the time I went to the airport, I had done enough drugs to kill the average dope fiend. I had also cried enough tears to fill a Sparklets bottle. As I went through the security check point I was pulled out of line and taken to a room to be searched. I had figured this would happen so I didn't bring any drugs with me for the trip. After they searched and found nothing, a cop asked me why I looked so bad? I explained to him about my sister dying and that I was going to Vegas to the funeral. He felt sorry for me and rushed me to the gate so I wouldn't miss my flight.

I arrived in Vegas a little after midnight and by the time I got my bag and took a cab to Derek's it was about 4:30 am. He let me in and hugged me. It was all I could do to not start crying again. After a pot of coffee and a shower we were both feeling and looking better. The limo arrived at 8:00am to take us to the cemetery.

It was an incredible service, I swear at least a thousand people showed up to say their goodbyes. Afterwards lunch was served at Peggy's house. It had been a while since all of that part of my family had seen me, so there was plenty for me not to tell everyone. Catch my drift?

By 2:00 pm I was on my way back to the airport and headed for home. I arrived at the house 30 minutes short of when I had left the day before. I was also coming down off of a three-day high. I dragged myself to the bedroom and got my gun out the safe. Then I laid down and slept for 40 straight hours.

It is pretty plain to see that something more had died inside of me because of my sister's passing. I am, however, unable to tell you exactly how I felt because I was so numb from all the dope and booze I had consumed during this period of time. I do recall being angry at Sister for leaving me here in this god-awful world to fend for myself. I guess it's true that only the good die young!

As we move on with the story, it was business as usual! But it wasn't long after the funeral that my connection got busted. So, there I was with this demand and no supply. This went on for several weeks. One morning, I got a call from my friend in jail. He gave me an address and told me to go there and that they were expecting me.

I knocked on the door and a woman answered. She was Mexican, but she spoke English very well. She explained to me that they had close to a ton of dope, but no one to sell it. She asked me how much I could sell on a daily basis. I told her I could easily sell a half pound, and if I hustled I could probably get rid of a pound. She smiled and said something to her husband in Spanish. After they went back and forth a few times, she looked at me and asked if I want to work with them. I readily agreed. She told me how they worked their deliveries and how I was to return the money to them. Then she gave me a zip lock bag that had a pound of meth in it and said, "I'll see you tomorrow."

Now for those of you who don't know, that pound of dope was worth $10,000 dollars, and I had to pay it back in 24 hours. I stood to make between $4-6,000 for myself, depending on how I sold it.

I was now THE MAN as they say in the dope game, and this was where I would stay for the next couple of years. I am not going to say much more than that on this subject. Mostly because I hate to glorify the fact that I was the man in charge of so much pain and suffering. It's nothing to be proud of, the way I spent my life in those years. I will end this chapter by saying, "Nothing you've seen in the movies about drugs comes close to describing the reality of the dangers and horrors of trafficking meth."

CHAPTER 19: YOU GOTTA LOVE FAMILY

There was a reason I had that sinking feeling when O'ma had come to bring the message about my sister passing away! You see, while O'ma was at my house she had seen some of my drug paraphernalia out on the coffee table. When she left my house, she went straight home and called my Uncle Ronnie. I don't know why she did that, except maybe she hoped he would talk to me about it.

That didn't make much sense to me, because Ronnie and I didn't really get along that great. I made an effort to just avoid him and keep the peace for O'mas sake. He had a bad habit of accusing me of fooling around with his wives. Yes, I said, "wives." He was now on his seventh wife and I had been accused of fooling around with all of them but Number One. With God as my witness, I had never done it, not once.

Number Seven, whose name was Dana, was only a couple of years older than me. She was a beautiful woman and she had a sweet spirit. I liked her and she liked me, but that was all there was to it. She was my aunt, by marriage to my uncle. Which made her family.

It came as no surprise to me that Ronnie showed up at my house to give me a lecture about drugs, and that I should quit before I got busted. Ronnie also told me then that he and Dana had split up and she wanted a divorce.

Now I won't get into all drama that I came to know about their problems, except to say that I knew what an asshole Ronnie could be. He was my father's brother, and neither acorn had fallen that far from the tree. They were in fact, peas of the same pod. I knew this from personal experience.

Anyway, I told Ronnie he should mind his own business. I had no intentions of quitting or of getting busted. I thanked him for his concern and said goodbye.

It wasn't that long after Ronnie had come by that there was a knock at my door. You have to understand that in my business a knock at the door without a phone call before-hand was met with a shot gun in my hand. Dana just froze when I opened the door. "Have I caught you at a bad time?" she asked.

I let her in and put my gun away. She looked tired, and I asked her if she was ok. She proceeded to tell me about all the reasons she was leaving my uncle, and then she explained that she had no money and that she had slept in her car for the last few nights because she had no place to go. I had figured it would be happening like this, because that was how Ronnie had treated the other six wives before her.

After she finished telling me all the gory details, I told her to go take a shower and change clothes. I knew this would make her relax and hopefully feel better. While she was in the shower, I made her something to eat. When she emerged from the bathroom she looked so much better than when she came in. I sat her down and watched her eat, and when she finished I told her to go lay down on my bed and get some sleep. I told her I had business to tend to and I would be in the garage for a couple of hours.

I had finished my business and decided to do some welding before I had to do my evening deliveries. While I was welding, Ronnie showed up and asked me where Dana was. I told him she was in the house asleep and that she was real upset about all fighting they had been doing. He said he needed to talk to her and went inside. I went back to my welding because I really didn't want to get involved in their drama any more than I already was.

It was only a couple minutes later that I heard a loud crash. I ran inside to see what was going on. As I entered my bedroom, Dana was getting up off the floor, her glasses were hanging off of one ear and the whole side of her face was red. Ronnie was standing over her with a look on his face that I had seen before. I immediately yelled at him to stop and to get out of my house. Ronnie turned to me and told me to go on and mind my own business. I yelled at him again to get out of my house and that he was not going to beat Dana up today. By this time, Dana was up off the floor and had stepped away from Ronnie's reach. The next thing I know Ronnie had pulled his .45 out of his coat and was pointing it at me. He insisted I leave the room again while he pointed his gun at me. I told him he was going to have to shoot me, because I was not going to let him beat her up in my house.

The next few seconds all happened in slow motion in my mind. Ronnie in his anger looked at me as he pulled the slide back on his gun to chamber a round. He pointed his gun straight at my chest and said, "OK, have it your way." As I looked in his eyes I knew he was going to shoot me right where I stood. I closed my eyes, Dana screamed, "NO!" and Ronnie pulled the trigger!

It was the damnedest thing I had ever encountered. The gun didn't fire, it just went click. I opened my eyes to see Ronnie trying to clear the bullet from the chamber, but it was jammed in there real tight. I took off down the hallway and grabbed my shotgun and turned and ran right back to my bedroom. I pointed the shotgun at Ronnie. I looked him straight in the eye and said, "This one doesn't misfire, you need to leave right now!"

After he was gone, I sat down and loaded a bowl to get high. Dana came over to me and hugged me and whispered in my ear that she was so glad I wasn't dead because of her. I just looked at her for moment, and then I asked, "What do you suppose the odds are of that gun misfiring?"
Now, I had had no belief in God up to this point in my life, but all I could come up with was divine intervention to explain what had just transpired. There was no other logical reason for it in my mind!

As you can imagine, the plot is about to thicken. As I sat there smoking my dope, my mind was racing about what to do next. I told Dana to help me clean house, which is a term that means get rid of all the drugs and paraphernalia in the house. Once the house was clean we called the police and when they got there, we filed charges against Ronnie for assault and attempted murder. On top of that I made Dana go to police station and file a Victim Protection Order against Ronnie.

The next few months were filled with all kinds of drama. I had decided that I had to help Dana get away from Ronnie. I put her up in a different hotel every couple of days, so she would be harder to find. I also gave her the money to file for the divorce, which we knew would be granted because Ronnie couldn't come to court since he had warrants out for his arrest. On top of that I gave her money so she could buy gas and food. All of this went on for several months.

It was during this time that I was taking care of all Dana's needs that I got to know her on a very personal level. No, I was not sleeping with her, but I had developed feelings for her. Feelings that I never once shared with anyone, especially her! I told myself that it was the right thing to do by helping her. If I didn't do it, no one would, and only God knows what might have happened to her.

CHAPTER 20: IT'S NEVER WRONG TO DO THE RIGHT THING

As I write this part of my story, you should know that if I had it to do all over, I would do the same thing again.

It was early one morning when I heard a knock at my door. When I looked through the peep hole, I saw Dana standing there on the other side. I opened the door and she came in.

"What's up," I said.

She was all nervous and fidgety, and she asked me to sit down and listen to what she had to say without interrupting. I did as she asked and sat down. She sat down right next to me and grabbed my hand. She looked me straight in the eyes and said, "I am in love with you and I want to be with you!"

Now what I felt when I heard those words is beyond my vocabulary to explain to you. I'm sure that I went into shock because I didn't say a word. A flood of emotions and thoughts ran through my mind and my heart at the same time.

"Well?" Dana asked me, still waiting for me to respond.

I never said anything, I just reached out and grabbed her and pulled her to me. I then I kissed her, long and slow. "I am in love with you too," I said.

The next thing I know, we were in bed making love. And it was making love, instead of having sex, I had never realized there was a difference until this moment.

Dana moved in on that day and I could not have possibly been any happier than I was when I was in her arms. And so it went that I did everything that I could to spoil her completely rotten. I would have bought her the moon, if it had been for sale! After a couple of months of playing house, I asked her to marry me and she said yes. The next day we got a marriage license and soon got married.

We put our heads together and made a plan for me to quit selling dope. You see, it's not that easy to quit working for the Mexican mob. They don't take kindly to people messing up their cash flow. As we began to put our plan in motion, the first step was to get married and then we would use our honeymoon as an excuse to leave town, and we would just keep on going. All I needed to do was put a little money together so we could get on our feet wherever we landed.

We were almost ready to make our move to a new life in another place, far from all the drama of the people I was wrapped up with in the dope game, to say nothing of our godawful families. Dana and I spent hours packing and planning all the things we planned to do when we were finally free from all the haters that wanted us to be as miserable as they were.

CHAPTER 21: I DIDN'T SEE THAT COMING

It was a Thursday night and I only had one delivery to make, and I was going to come home and make dinner. It was going to be just the two of us, a little candle light, soft music, good food, and romance.

As I left the house, a car was following me. I took off on my bike and it was still chasing me. I was cornered in a parking lot when they finally identified themselves as police. They put me under arrest and drove me back to my house. As I sat in the back seat watching them, ten more unmarked cars pulled up. They surrounded the house and then used the batter ram on my front door. This was around 8:30 in the evening, and they spent the next six hours tearing my house apart. After they had found all they could, they pulled me out of the car and tried to get me to rat on the people I got my dope from. I refused to tell them because I knew if I did that mine and Dana's lives would be over before the week was finished.

They finally took me downtown and booked me about 4:30 am on Friday morning. I had only been in my cell for a couple of hours when the door opened and they took me back downstairs and let me go. It just so happened that my bond agent was one of my customers and she had seen me getting booked in. I was released and I walked home which was about five miles from the jail.

As you might imagine, me getting arrested put Dana in quite a mood. After reading all the paper work the police had left and what I was given at the jail, it seemed that all I was charged with was possession of meth. This would slow our plans down a bit, but everything was still doable.

When we went to court a couple of weeks later was when it all hit the fan. All I was supposed to do was plead on the possession charge, but when I got up to stand in front of the judge's bench, the bailiff took me into custody again. The next thing I knew I was being booked on ten felonies and four misdemeanors. My bond was now set at $74,000. Dana was right on top of things, and she made all the calls to the people I worked for and to the various friends I had that would have enough money to bail me out.

To make this long story short, I was released a couple of days later. When I got to the house I went into the back yard and dug up the money that I owed my friend for bailing me out. Then, I went looking for a lawyer!

Now finding a lawyer wasn't nearly as hard as finding Dana. All of this drama was just too much for her, and she had taken off. Now I was all alone to face the music, so to speak.

I didn't blame her for leaving, but that doesn't mean it was easy to take. We had been through so much, in such a short time. The thought of prison was just too much for her I suppose! As it turns out, she was smart to run off.

When I went to talk to my lawyer, he told me that they had filed on Dana. She had warrants for all the same charges that I had been arrested for. He also told me how I had gotten on the watch list of the police. It was my dear uncle Ronnie who had ratted me out. Apparently, he was still pissed about not getting to shoot me and probably even more pissed that I had married his ex-wife! We will talk about that a little later.

My lawyer then told me that if I talked to Dana, I should convince her to turn herself in. We would make arrangements with a bondsman so she wouldn't have to go to jail. She would just get booked and then let out on bond. That is just what happened when I finally caught up with her.

As soon as Dana's walk through was done, we went to see the lawyer that my lawyer had recommended we use to represent Dana. After talking with her, she agreed to represent Dana as soon as we paid the fee. I told her I had it right then and I got up and handed it to her. She was real nice and she thanked me for the fee that I had just paid, then she told Dana to come by tomorrow and they would talk about her case.

What a snake that lawyer was! The first thing she did was file for an annulment of our marriage. She told Dana to stay away from me at all costs. This was how she would sell the story to a judge, by lying and telling the judge that Dana had no knowledge of me dealing drugs, and that getting our marriage annulled was Dana's idea to distance herself from me. Then she lied to Dana, telling her that she would be able to get all the charges dropped if she did what she told her to do.

That is the just of how it all went down. I will tell you that none of it set well with me! But there wasn't a thing that I could do about it except cry!

CHAPTER 22: MY DESCENT INTO HELL

As I begin to write this chapter, I am filled with all kinds of emotions. I have only just begun to write and the tears are rolling down my face.

It is here, in this story, that all my mistakes in life have finally caught up with me. Even the things I did right will no longer be of any benefit. And it is not so much the things that happen, but instead, the way they affected me emotionally and psychologically that make this so hard to tell you.

Dana, the love of my life is gone, I am now homeless, and I am out on a $74,000 bond. All that I have left in this world is my van and some clothes. I also have some money, but after paying the bondsman and lawyers, what I had left is barely enough to live on for a few months. I can't even sell any more dope because I already owe the Mexicans 10k that the police confiscated. I was also warned by my lawyer not to get caught selling any more dope or he wouldn't be able to help me.

The days went by, each day the same as the one before. All I could do was get high and try not to think about what was coming. But I was only fooling myself, because it was coming, and I was running out of time.

After a couple months of living this way, if you could even call it living, I had to appear in court. As I sat with my lawyer, we discussed the charges against me. It wasn't until the district attorney was done talking that I realized how bad my situation really was.

LIFE! In prison! That was what the DA was asking for in regards to my charges.

My lawyer told me that, it seemed to him, the DA was trying to make an example out me. But the really bad news was that the judge I was in front of was known for being especially hard on drug dealers. With ten felonies and four misdemeanors, it was highly unlikely that the judge wouldn't follow the recommendations of the DA.

I was so glad when court was finally over! After the judge had left the room, my lawyer told me that I needed to take care of anything and everything that was pressing in my pitiful life, turn myself in to the bondsman and go to jail. He told me that I was going to go to prison, for how long was the only thing he could help me with at this point. He explained to me that I would get credit for the time I was in jail when they sentenced me. That same time would also give him something to work with as a bargaining chip for some of the lesser charges. I told him that I understood and would do as he said.

As I left the court house, feeling morally bankrupt, my thoughts were all about what the DA had said. Did I really want to spend the rest of my life in prison? Most certainly I did not! And, for the first time in my life I was no longer looking for a way to get out of my troubles. Instead, I was looking for a way to end them.

It wasn't that big of a leap to suicide. I had already lost everything that I loved or cared about, I was homeless, I was only a couple hundred dollars from broke, and I was facing life in prison.

I was deep into depression by the end of that day, but it wasn't until my phone rang that I finally hatched a plan to end it all. One of my customers wanted to trade his prescription of pain killers for a 1/16 of meth. As luck would have it, I had the 1/16 of dope. I agreed to trade and drove to meet him. After our deal was done, I went to the liquor store and bought a bottle of whiskey. Then, I went back to my friend's house to get my things and my dog. Her name was Mrs. and she was all that I had left in this world to love. It is only now, as I write this, that I understand why it was so important for me to get her. I didn't want to die alone!

By the time I had reached the place where I planned to do the deed, I had finished smoking the last of my meth. It was late in the afternoon and the sun was low on the horizon. I was miles away from civilization as I stopped the van and opened the back door.

Mrs. jumped out to check things out and take care of her business. I threw everything out of the van and made a pallet in the back to lay on. I crawled inside and grabbed the bottle of whiskey along with the pills that I had traded for. I opened the pill bottle and poured all 90 of them into my mouth. Then I washed them down with the bottle of whiskey. I sat there in the back of the van petting Mrs. while I watched the sunset. As the whiskey and pills started to do their job, it was impossible to hold myself up. So, I laid down and held on to my dog as I waited for death to come!

CHAPTER 23: I CAN'T DO ANYTHING RIGHT!

Boy, was I pissed off when I woke up three days later. I was also sick as hell! As I was puking, just outside of my van, I was cursing God at the top of my lungs.

I just couldn't understand how I was still alive.

I got myself pulled together as best I could, and I drove to a friend's house. He took one look at me and shook his head. He told me to come in and offered me something to eat and drink. I told him what I had done and that I was too sick to eat, but I would take a beer if he had one.

While I drank the beer, I put Mrs. in the back yard and fed her. Then I called my connection and asked for a front. He knew right away that something was really wrong since I never asked for a front. I always paid cash. He said that he had some dope and that I could come and get what I needed to get my head right. I told my friend that I would be back in a little bit and left to get my dope.

I never made it there! I ran out of gas on the way and a cop pulled up to check if I needed help. I told him that I had tried to kill myself and I just wanted to turn myself in like my lawyer had told me to. After he ran my license, he agreed with me and took me in.

When we got to the jail, I went through the usual booking process, until we got to the part where you have to put on your orange monkey suit. I forgot that I had told the police about trying to kill myself. So, instead of general population, I was lucky enough to be going to segregation. This is where they take you if they think you are going to hurt yourself on their watch. Instead of the orange jumpsuit, they strip you naked and put you in a green straight jacket. This is called the turtle suit, unaffectionately, by those unlucky enough to get to wear one. It is just long enough to cover your unmentionables, yet short enough that you can sit on the toilet and do your business, except for the paper work of course. It is impossible to do the paper work in a straight-jacket, just in case you didn't know! Oh yeah, one more thing you should know, it is not a padded room they put you in. It is a six foot by six foot room with a cement floor, a cement slab to lay on, and cement block walls. All of which are painted light grey so you will remain calm. If you are fortunate enough to not sit and dwell on who was in the room before you, and what kind of disgusting body fluid they managed to rub, wipe, puke, or just deposit on the exact place you are trying to lay your head to sleep.

Anyway, I'm sure you get the picture. And this is how I spent the first 48 hours of my incarceration. When the psychiatrist finally came to see me, I begged him to put me in general population. I couldn't have been happier when they brought me my orange monkey suit.

I cannot describe how good the shower felt after two days in a turtle suit laying on God only knows what! And the matt they gave me to lay on felt like a pillow top mattress after that cement slab. Regardless of these wonderful luxuries that I was given, I was still in jail and on my way to prison.

CHAPTER 24: JAIL IS ALSO A FOUR-LETTER WORD

This chapter will span a period of just over eight months. There are many aspects of life in jail, few of which are pleasant. Having said that, I must also tell you that even though it is not a pleasant place, there is still good that can come from the experience.

I suppose the best thing about going to jail is the chance to dry out of whatever substance you have been abusing, or should I say whatever substance has been abusing you? It is a lot easier to put things in perspective when you're not messed up on drugs or alcohol.

Perspective can mean several things, but for me, it was helpful to sit and think about my situation without the stress of having to try to survive at the same time. Perspective can come from someone else's opinion who is in a similar situation. This was definitely true for me when I met Johnny. He was the first person that I met when I got sent to general population. He was an interesting character who was a few years older than me and a bit of an enigma. He was the only person in the pod that was bold enough to talk to me. He was also a good listener, which was exactly what I needed during this most upsetting of times. I will classify my meeting Johnny as another divine intervention in my life, and you will understand why as we move forward with this story.

There I was locked in cell with at least one other guy, but there were times that it would be two other guys. For those that have never been in jail, the cells are 8' by 10' with a 10' ceiling. There are two steel beds mounted to the wall and a toilet and a shelf mounted on the other side. That is not a lot space to share with one stranger, let alone two. There is nothing to do except sleep or sit and talk to your cellie. They would let us out of our cells for a couple of hours every day to shower and exercise. This was when I would talk with Johnny. We would walk back and forth around the pod and just talk about whatever was on our minds. Much of the time we just talked about what we missed from our lives before we got busted. Other times we talked about what might happen at our next court appearance. That's all there was to do, just walk and talk, and take a shower. It was, however, the best 2 hours of each day. The other 22 were the challenge to get through. Being locked in that cell all day, every day, was enough to drive you insane!

I wasn't there long before I figured out that reading was a great way to pass the time, if you could find a book. I also took up drawing on envelopes to pass the time and to get food. I drew all kinds of cartoons and flowers, and I even designed tattoos for those who chose prison as a way of life. I would then trade my drawings for items of food that my fellow inmates would buy from the canteen. This is how I managed not to starve to death while I was locked in jail.

Now for most, losing a few pounds would be considered another good thing about going to jail, but for me it was a lot more than just a few pounds. I weighed 255 pounds when I went in, and within four months I was down to 195 pounds. I looked like a skeleton with some skin stretched over it.

And so it goes, the wheels of justice turn slowly, but they do turn. After months of waiting, my day in court was finally approaching. I had managed to survive for about six months without going completely nuts. You see, when you're locked up, you go through many mental changes, or should I say phases.

You start with denial, not wanting to even face the fact that you are in jail. Then comes anger, you're mad at everything and everyone that was part of you ending up in jail. Then for some, there is the hope of being released. For the rest, there is acceptance of what is going to be, which is prison.

I was right on borderline of anger and acceptance when my lawyer came to see me before I went to court. The first words out of his mouth when he saw me were, "Jesus, don't they feed you in here!" I told him that I was doing all I could to not starve to death, but I had already lost 65 pounds, and if I kept losing at the same rate I was losing now I would be dead in about another six months.

He told me that that would not happen because I would be in prison long before six months. Lucky me!

He then told me to sit down while he explained what was going to be my best option for court. He said I would need to do a blind plea so that the DA will have no say in the amount of time I have to serve, which we already know they are seeking a life sentence. So, cutting them from the equation is going to be the best thing you can do. Then he tells me the bad news.

If you do the blind plea, it means that you are willing to except whatever the judge gives you as a sentence. You cannot appeal his decision in court.

It was at this time that I had come to full acceptance of my situation. I was going to prison for a very long time, and, in fact, my life was over. Now I didn't tell my lawyer what I was thinking, but just agreed with his plan. We finished our talk and I returned to my cell.

It was about this same time that Johnny went to court. He was there for trafficking marijuana. I'll never forget the look on his face when he told me that they gave him a 10-year sentence. He was already in his late fifties and 10 years just sucked the life right out of him. It also sucked the life right out of me because I had 13 more charges than Johnny. We walked and talked for the last time that day. We said our goodbyes and wished each other luck.

I went to court a couple of weeks later to finally be sentenced. I remember feeling sick to my stomach as I sat in the court room waiting my turn to see the judge. I felt like I had to poop and throw up at the same time, but neither would happen even when I tried to let it go. The anticipation was going to kill me, even if my sentence didn't.

When they called my name, I stood up and walked to the table in front of the judge's bench. My lawyer joined me and stood to my right. There was a lot of talking back and forth, but I couldn't follow what was being said. Finally, the judge asked me if I understood what I was about to do? I told him that I did.

The judge started reading my charges and giving sentence to each at the same time. I was unable to follow what was being said because he spoke so fast and I was so scared, and felt so sick to my stomach. All I heard him say was three tens and a five, and in my condition, it took me a minute to even add that up in my head. When I finally got to the number 35 in my head, my knees buckled and I had to lean on the table to hold myself up. A sentence of 35 years meant that I would be 79 years old when I got out, if I happened to live that long.

The judge asked me if I had anything that I wanted to say. I looked him straight in the eye and answered, "Yes, I do." I paused for just a second before I began to speak. As I opened my mouth to say my piece, it was as if the whole world had come to a total stop. "Your honor, I am guilty of all the things that I was charged with, and a bunch more that I was not. I understand that it is your job to see that I pay my debt to society as it is laid out in the law. But you should know that what you're doing to me is in no way part of my punishment for the things that I have done wrong. I have already received my punishment and learned my lesson through the loss of all things that I hold dear or have ever cared about in my life. Because of drugs I have lost my family, my wife, my dog, my home, all my worldly possessions, and finally my self-respect. I have already learned my lesson, so now, I will pay my debt to society!"

As I finished speaking, the world started to spin again. My lawyer and the judge were talking and the judge had his hand over the microphone. When he took his hand away from the mic, he looked at me and asked the clerk to give him a date for me to return to court in a year's time. Once the date was given, he ordered that I be brought back in front of him on that day. "We will talk again next April," he said, and out the door I went!

I got back to the jail just in time for dinner. I'm not sure how I managed to eat my food, because I still felt sick. Right after dinner was when they let us out to exercise and shower. A lot of guys that I had come to know came around to ask me what my sentence was. I told them all about what had happened, and how many years I was to serve. One of the guys I had gone to court with came over and gave me a cup of coffee. It was his way of saying how bad he felt for me getting a 35-year sentence.

After our time in the pod was over, we all went back to our cells. The guard told me to pack up my stuff because I was going upstairs to the Department of Corrections pod. That was where you waited to pull chain.

CHAPTER 25: PRISON ISN'T A FOUR-LETTER WORD, BUT IT SHOULD BE!

Now for those that don't know what pulling chain is, all I can tell you is it means waiting for them to take you to prison. I remember someone telling a romantic story about where the term comes from, but I can't remember the story. Besides, there is nothing romantic about prison!

I arrived upstairs to a pod full of guys all waiting to be taken to prison. The rules for prisoners in this pod were way different from where I had just come from. For starters, there were less people, so you never shared a room with more than one person. If you didn't give the guards any trouble, they would let you choose your own cellie. That evening, the door swung open and there stood the most muscle-bound guy I had seen in a long time. I couldn't help but think of all the movies I had watched where the big guy comes in and makes his cellie into his girlfriend. Thank God it didn't happen like that on this occasion.

He walked in, dropped his stuff on the bottom bunk, stood up and stretched out his hand to shake mine. "I'm Robert," he said. "What's your name?"

I shook his hand and told him my name. "You're not a serial killer are you? he asked with a smile on his face.

I liked him already. He made me laugh on one of the worst days of my life. It felt good to laugh, and it sure did the mood in our cell a lot of good.

As he went about settling in, we engaged in the usual small talk that takes place every time you get a new cellie. Finally, his rack was made up and he had put all of his items from the canteen on the shelf next to the toilet. I couldn't help but notice that he had a lot of canteen, so I asked him if he was here for robbing a store? We both laughed again and continued on with our small talk.

I was on the top rack drawing on an envelope the whole time he was going on about his day in court. He stopped mid-sentence to get a closer look at what I was doing. "Hey that's pretty good art work," he said. "How much do you sell them for?"

I told him a dollar each, and he asked if I had any more. I showed him what I had finished and he took a good look at each one and put them on the shelf by his canteen. "I'll take all of them," he said. Just get what you want for them out of that stuff on the shelf over there. I couldn't believe my luck, it usually took me a week to sell that many. So, I jumped down from my rack and went shopping, and then I jumped back up and started eating a candy bar.

Since my painted envelopes helped me survive, I want to explain how. A prisoner's contact with the outside world typically consists of letters to friends and family. An envelope with high quality artwork was a huge luxury to send to a loved one. My artwork was excellent, plus I found ways to "paint" them with food dye, so my envelopes were unique.

Robert made us both a cup of coffee and we sat and shot the breeze for quite a while. The lights went out at 11 pm, so we both laid down on our racks and went to sleep. I remember thinking about all that had happened over the course of that day as I laid there falling asleep. I couldn't get over the 35 years I was going to serve, but on the other hand, I really wasn't that upset about it. It is only now that I come to realize that I was just glad that I didn't have to keep living in the turmoil that was my life before I was put in this place.

As you can imagine, Robert and I came to be good friends. He was just as dumb as a rock, but never had a bad thing to say. All he did was work out and drink coffee, which was fine by me since he always made two cups. Having a cellie like him made that month before I pulled chain a whole lot more bearable.

Another thing that made it easier to accept my fate, was that during this month of waiting, Dana was to go to court for her sentencing. Of course, I already knew what her sentence would be, because her sentence was included in my sentence. You see, I had worked it out with my lawyer as part of my doing a blind plea. The judge had agreed to drop all of Dana's charges except for one, possession of Controlled Dangerous Substance. Dana was to receive only five years of probation.

My lawyer had worked this out for me against his better judgement. He felt that Dana going along with her lawyer's plan was just a little crappy. He felt like she should have owned up to her part in my getting busted. I told him that I was still in love with her, and I didn't want her to have to go to prison. Besides, what purpose would be served in two people doing time for the same crimes?

On the day that Dana went to court, I received a note from my lawyer telling me that the judge kept his word and Dana received five years of probation. I was filled with warm fuzzy thoughts because I had done what I thought was the right thing to do. And, you have to understand that after all the bad decisions that I had made in the past, it felt pretty good to do something right. But even those warm fuzzy thoughts wouldn't be enough to get me through what was about to happen later that evening.

Right after dinner we had what they call "count time." This is when the guards count the inmates to make sure that no one has wandered off when no one was watching. While they do the count, they tell those inmates that have visitors waiting to get ready. When the guard told me I had a visitor, I almost fell off of my rack. My stomach rolled over and I almost crapped my pants. Literally. I was sitting on the toilet when the guard opened my cell door. He told me to hurry up because everyone was waiting on me.

I went in the room, and walked one-by-one to each window until I came to the one where Dana was sitting, waiting on me. I couldn't help myself and I started to cry. Dana tried to calm me down and it worked to some degree. As we sat and talked for the first time since this whole mess got started, I was filled with so many emotions that it was hard to talk.

Dana thanked me for what I had done to keep her out of prison. She told me that she loved me and how sorry she was that I was going to prison. After hearing her say those things and seeing her face-to-face while she said them, all those warm fuzzy feelings came back. I stopped crying and we sat and talked until my time was up. It wasn't until I got back to my cell that I started to cry again.

Robert got up and fixed us both a cup of coffee, then looked at me as he handed me mine. He said, "You need to stop that crying and never do it again. If you cry in prison they will consider you weak, and they will make your time locked up a living hell. That is free advice from someone who knows." Then he sat on toilet and asked me what Dana and I had talked about.

As I sat and drank my coffee, I told Robert everything about my visit. He listened and seemed to be happy for me that she had come to see me. As he was making us another cup of coffee, the guards opened our door so we could hit the pod until it was time for bed. We were walking through the door as he grabbed my shoulder and reminded me of what he had told me earlier, never cry again until you're free!

That was my last night in jail. My name was called to pull chain about 2 am the next morning. It was a long process that you had to go through to finally get on the bus that took you to A&R. But, as the bus got on the highway, I couldn't help but notice the sun was coming up over the horizon, and I could feel the breeze of cool morning air on my face and in my hair. The radio on the bus was playing a song that I liked and I started singing along with the radio. I felt alive for the first time in almost nine months!

CHAPTER 26: A & R DOES NOT MEAN "ACTION AND RELAXATION"

Here I was, riding down the road on my way to the Big House. It is a strange feeling that comes over you as you realize that this is where you will live from now on. Big ugly buildings all painted grey with miles of fencing, to say nothing of the endless amounts of razor wire. All of this for little ole me!

A & R is just a place they take you to while they figure out which prison to send you to. They do this by calculating how many times you have been in, what your current charges are, how much time you received, and if you are connected to any gangs. This is usually determined by the tattoos that you have on your body and, last of all, if you have a problem with violence.

They take you to see every kind of doctor there is to determine what medicines you may require or if you have disabilities. After they have all of this info and they are done humiliating you, they decide which yard you will go to when the next bus comes by. All of this was done, in my case, in nine days. And a funny thing that you should know, was that even though I had all of those bad charges, it was the fact that I didn't have any tattoos that allowed me to go to a minimum-security prison.

There is not much else to say about all of this, except that it was not a pleasant experience. I would not recommend it to my worst enemy!

CHAPTER 27: I FINALLY MADE IT

I arrived at my yard on a Friday afternoon. I was taken in and put in a cell, where they left me until Monday morning. It was around 10 am when the sergeant took me out of the prison fence and pointed to a dirt road. He said, "Follow that road until you find someone who cares that you are here."

I thought to myself that is was a strange thing to say to a man that just got handed 35 years to serve. I was outside the fence, and he had no intentions of walking me to where I was supposed to be, and I didn't have on any handcuffs or shackles.

As I followed the road around the corner, I realized that I was only 50 yards from the freeway. This all seemed a lot strange to me, so I walked a little faster and quit looking at that freeway. As I got to the top of the hill, the road ended, right in front of a building. I opened the door and there sat a guard. He yelled to me, "Who are you and why are you standing in my office during count time?" I told him my name and that the sergeant from next door told me to come around that road until I found someone who cared I was here.

The sergeant I was talking to was named Franks, and he told me to give him a minute to finish the count and then he would deal with me. When he announced that the count was clear, suddenly there were inmates going in all directions. He yelled at one and told him to get me the stuff I needed to make up my rack, and to get me some clothes to wear. He showed me to the rack that was to be mine, and I went to work putting it together and storing my stuff in my locker. Sergeant Franks then told me that I was to work in the kitchen serving the food and that it was my responsibility to be ready to go to work after the count cleared before each meal of the day.

By the time I had taken care of my stuff and answered a thousand questions by other inmates, it was time for the dinner count. As the guard came through, he yelled for kitchen help to come with him. I followed him to the mess hall, where I was given my apron and net for my hair. All the food came in from across the fence in big cabinets on wheels. Then, we would set it all up to serve my fellow inmates as they came though the line.

I was scared to death, and had no idea what the hell was going on. I just kept my head down and scooped the green beans on to each tray as it passed by. I had not been there very long when I heard my name called out from in front of me. When I looked up, there was Johnny! He said to me, "I'll see you after dinner in the yard".

After dinner, I went out to the yard and found my old friend. We had a lot to talk about. So much had happened since the last time we talked in jail. I remember thinking how lucky I was to already have a friend to talk to, and hopefully fill me in on how things worked around this place.

As you can imagine, Johnny and I were right back in a rhythm, just like we were in jail. We both did our jobs each day and then all of our free time was spent together, walking and talking, just like before.

It didn't take long to figure out that prison was way better than jail. Believe it or not, you had way more freedom in prison. The only real problem that I could see, was that you had to pay attention to everything you did, so as not to piss anyone off. Doing that could be hazardous to your health! The thing to remember in prison is that every person you deal with is a potential train wreck. You have to pick your acquaintances carefully, and chose your friends even more carefully. The less people you chill with, the less bullshit you deal with! Got it?

Other than these few simple things that you had to pay attention to, prison wasn't that bad. Don't get me wrong, it wasn't that great either.. The thing was, you just had to come to terms with the whole situation. This was your life, and once you learned to deal with that, you could live one day at a time. Even when the days seemed to go on endlessly.

Where I struggled was in the thoughts that I had where I told myself there was HOPE. Hope is a terrible thing to have in prison! Hope will literally destroy you in prison if you let it. This I tell you from experience.

I set in to prison life without too many problems. I was fortunate to have Johnny as my friend, and I was fortunate to have a job in the kitchen. And, there are those who would say that I was fortunate to be alive, but I had had not come to believe that yet.

I was also fortunate the day that Johnny and I got to be cellies. We were in an area called the dungeon. It used to be that this place was jail inside of prison, if you can believe that. Now, however, it was just used as rooms to store inmates. There were only five rooms in this area, and they all had their own toilets and there was a shower that had to be shared with those in that area. Sharing a shower with nine other guys was way better than sharing with 99 other guys. Best of all, it was underground, so it was cooler in the summer and warmer in the winter.

CHAPTER 28: A TIME OF LEARNING

Believe it or not, a man can learn a lot in prison. In this chapter, I will attempt to tell you of all the things that I learned either by my myself, or with the help of my friend Johnny.

I suppose the most important thing you learn is survival. People think that the guards run the prisons, but that is not true. The inmates run the prisons. The guards are just there to count you and to make sure you get fed three times a day. The rules of engagement are set forth by the inmates. The sooner you learn these rules the better off you are. Pissing off the wrong person can be hazardous to your health. If something doesn't concern you, leave it alone. Never point or stare at another inmate, and don't use the words bitch or punk unless you are ready to fight. Last of all, nothing is free in prison.

Reading is a great way to learn and prisons always have a decent library. While I was locked up, I'm sure I read at least 300 books. Funny thing though, the Bible is the most read book in prison. I found that to be quite ironic.

When you are locked up, you will learn not to be in a hurry. NOTHING happens fast in prison. You are there to do time, and plenty of it. I remember someone telling me to do your time, don't let your time do you. This little bit of advice was one of the hardest things to learn, at least for me!

Some prisons even have schools in them. An inmate can actually study and get a GED. I even met a few that were taking college courses. Then, there are the programs that you can get in, if you're lucky or court ordered. Most of the guys in these programs don't learn much though, because if they had learned something, they wouldn't keep coming back to prison.

CHAPTER 29: LETTERS AND LIFE

In the last two chapters I gave you a bunch of general information, but now I would like to get back to my actual story. So, where was I? Oh yeah, I was fortunate to be cellies with Johnny, down in the dungeon.

By the time I got moved in with Johnny, my mail had finally caught up with me. There were letters from Dana and a letter from my mom.

The letter from my mom was a response to the letter I had sent her from jail. I had written her to tell her that I was going to prison. I just wanted her to hear it from me. I thought that that would be better than her hearing it through the grape vine. After the third letter I received from her, our communication was breaking down. She was upset that I was in prison, and she had every right to be upset. I, however, was the one in prison and I didn't want to hear any lectures about mistakes that I had made to end up in prison. In my last letter to her, I told her that if she couldn't say anything nice, to just stop writing. So, she did! I never got another letter from her. To this day, I have not been in communication with her although I have tried very hard to do so.

Which brings me to the letters from Dana. I know that I told you how much I loved Dana, but I will tell you again! Or maybe not! What can I say, that hasn't already been said? My whole body ached to be with her, and it was as if I was bleeding to death every time I read her letters. She would always spray them with the perfume that I had bought her, and she would always sign them with a red kiss in lipstick. It was like shaving my head with a cheese grater when I read her letters. All the sweet things she would say to me in them only made me bleed that much more. And then, there were no more letters. She had given up, and I laid down on my rack and died. And that is where I stayed for almost a month. I wouldn't do anything but lay there and stare out the window.

I stared for hours, that turned to days, that turned to weeks, and by the time they were fixing to turn to months, Johnny had had enough. Yes, it was my friend who helped me up, or should I say down, since I lived on the top bunk. Either way, there would be no more mourning in our cell. And now you might understand what I meant when I told you that hope is a killer when your locked up!

All my ties to the outside world were gone. I was just a number in a warehouse full of convicts. I only mattered to one person, and that was Johnny.

We were as close as two men can be, just short of being gay. We spent hours talking, and when he started going to church, we spent hours talking about that. He would go to Bible study every Monday night. When he got back, I would go on and on at him about how stupid he was to buy into all that crap about God. We argued back and forth about it almost every day. So finally, Johnny said to me, "Why don't you come with me and ask Ron all those questions you have?"

That is what I did. I went there just to disrupt the class with all my questions about God. And guess what? I ended up actually learning something that night. I went back the next week, and the week after that. Before I knew it, I was looking forward to class every Monday night. After a while, Monday wasn't enough, so I started doing Bible studies during the week in my cell. After a few months of this, I began to feel like a Phoenix, rising from the ashes of my once pathetic life. It was time for me to join the living once again.

Then one morning, Franks yelled to Johnny, "Pack your stuff! You're going out on the bus to another yard." This freaked both of us out. Johnny packed his stuff and was gone in about 20 minutes. And I was left alone again.

I didn't know it then, but God had begun to work in our lives. I had come far enough out of the ashes to stand on my own. So, I continued to go to Bible study, and I continued to do my studying in my cell. Ron brought news to me about Johnny. He told me that Johnny had gone to a sentence review and they had cut his time in half. His sentence was just for five years now, and he would be eligible for parole soon. This was good news, and not just for Johnny. I had one of these reviews coming up in a couple of month or so. What could happen at my review was all I could think about. Once again, I had hope, and once again it was killing me. The clock was my worst enemy, because time just seems to stop when you are waiting for something like a review.

The day finally came, and Franks yelled to me, just like he had done to Johnny. I got on that bus and never looked back as it drove off. The ride took hours because we drove to three other yards to pick up other inmates who were being transported to various other places. When I arrived at my new yard it was already night time, and the yard was locked down for the night. They gave me my bedding and took me to the building where I was to stay.

I couldn't believe my eyes when I walked through the door. It was a big open warehouse with beds all over the place. Inmates were everywhere, and they all seemed to be staring at the new guy, me. My new cellie introduced himself and as politely as he could, told me that I needed a shower. I agreed with him, but I didn't have my box of belongings yet, so I didn't have my shower gear. He loaned me some soap and a towel so I could shower. When I got back to my bunk, all clean and smelling better, he asked me if I was hungry. I told him I was and he gave me a ramen to eat. I finished my noodles and cleaned his bowl, then laid down on my rack and fell asleep.

The next morning at breakfast, there was Johnny. It was so good to see him, and once again we had a lot to talk about!

CHAPTER 30: THE BIG REVIEW

I barely had time to get settled in at the new yard before it was time to go to my judicial review. It was April 1, and all I could think about was it being Fool's Day. Lucky for me it was just another day in the eyes of the court.

When we arrived at the court house, they took me upstairs to the room that I was to see the judge. We were there a little early, so I had to wait for my turn. When my lawyer finally showed up, court was already in session. There was a big case being heard before the judge I was to see. The guy on trial had killed two small children in an accident in which he just so happened to be both drunk and high. The judge that I was to see had just sentenced this guy to life in prison. My lawyer decided that this was not the day for me to see the judge, on account of the fact he would be in a lousy mood after sending that guy to prison for life because he killed two kids. My lawyer got up and left the court house. When the judge got to my name on the docket, he asked me where my lawyer was? I told him that I didn't know. The judge said that he couldn't review my case without my lawyer present, so he set my court date for the following Friday, and back to the yard I went.

Now I had been waiting for this review for a year, but waiting for this next week was nothing short of torture. All I did was speculate on what the outcome would be. When I was sure I had it figured out, I would think of something else and change my mind completely. The truth of the matter was that I had no idea what was going to happen.

The next Friday morning finally came and I had that same sick feeling in my gut that I had on the day that I was sentenced. The drive to the courthouse only took an hour or so, but it seemed so much longer as I sat in the back seat wearing handcuffs and shackles. When we arrived at our destination, we went upstairs to the same courtroom that I had been in before. Only this time, we were the only people in the room. We sat for about an hour before my lawyer finally showed up. I stood up to shake his hand and I asked him where everyone was? He told me everything was fine, and that the judge and DA were in the next room waiting for him to go in.

We sat down to talk and my lawyer asked me if I had been staying out of trouble. I told him that I had been a perfect angel for the last year. He gave me a sideways look as if he didn't believe me. The guard that had brought me to court handed my jacket to my lawyer and said, "He is telling you the truth, see for yourself."

"That's just what I wanted to hear," my lawyer said, "Let's see if I can get you out of here today." Then, my lawyer got up and went into the room where the judge and DA were supposed to waiting. The guard and I sat there waiting for what seemed like an eternity. In reality it was only about five minutes. When my lawyer came back through the door, my stomach rolled over and I thought I might be sick. The stress of this was just killing me.

As my lawyer sat back down, he tells me that he has good news and bad news and which did I want first? I looked him straight in the eyes and said, "I'm not going home today because they can't balance suspend on a trafficking charge, so what is the good news?"

My lawyer said, "I see that you have done your homework, so here is the good news. I got them to lower all three 10-year sentences to their minimums, which is 4 years, and I got them to run all of your charges concurrent. With the time that you have already served, you are eligible for parole immediately. Worst case scenario is that you will only have to serve two more years if you didn't make parole."

As he finished telling me about the good news, I leaned back in my chair and I took a deep breath. A smile came across my face as I did the math in my head. I didn't know if I should laugh or cry, it was all so overwhelming. I grabbed his hand again and shook it while, I thanked him from the bottom of my heart.

"You did one hell of job," I said.

"You still have to talk the judge," he said, "but it's just a formality."

It was only a minute or two before the clerk came in and said, "All rise." The judge entered the room and took a seat, followed closely by the DA.

My lawyer and I walked over to the judge and stood there waiting for him to speak. When he had finished looking at my jacket, he took off his glasses and looked at me.

"It seems you are a man of your word," he said.

I was unable to speak, so I nodded my head instead.

"I am going to reduce all your charges to their minimum and I am going to run them concurrent," he said, "and I would hope that you will continue to do your best, both during your remaining time and when you are released. Good luck to you sir!"

And that was that! I was given my life back with the stroke of a pen!

CHAPTER 31: LIKE A PHOENIX

I was back to the yard by mid-afternoon. I couldn't wait to tell Johnny all about the day that I had just had. As we sat and talked, I told him all that I have just told you. Johnny and I both laughed to each other and we decided that it was cause for a celebration. Johnny went to his locker and got a nutty bar and a Dr. Pepper. When he came back, we sat and shared the treats that we both loved so dearly. Now, I'm not sure which one of us it was, but we had the thought of when would we go in front of the parole board?

There we were, both back to having hope, and it was killing both of us. A funny thing happened though, both of our jackets came back to our case workers at the same time. This meant that we would be on the same list to go in front of the parole board.

I don't remember all the details about how and when Johnny was called, but I can tell you how it went for me. My review was on April 8, and I was called in front of the parole board on June 21, and I found out that I had made parole on June 28. There was a stipulation, however, that I was to complete a program course before they would send my jacket to the Governor's office.

I had to wait over a month until they started that course again. The good news was that I could not be bumped from the course, because it was court ordered.

Life inside of prison went on, day by day, the same as it always had except for one thing. The yard that Johnny and I were at had church almost every night of the week. We both were still very much involved in seeking out God. We both had learned a lot about the Bible, and we both knew that God was working in our lives. What we didn't know was to what degree he was working. So, we just kept on going to church and we kept on learning about the Bible.

It was on August 7 that I got baptized in prison. Ron, the prison minister that I had first met at my last yard, also taught Bible study at the yard where we were currently serving our time. He was the one that baptized me on that day.

It was a strange feeling that I had when I came up out of the water. I was cleansed of my sins, free in Christ, and locked up in prison all at the same time. It was at this same time that I did a lot of soul searching. I had decided that I needed to make a bunch of changes in my life so that I would not end up being the same lost soul that I was before I came to prison. I had decided that I would never go back to my old life no matter how bad things got. I was a new man in the eyes of God, having just been baptized. I needed to set forth on a new path in life when I was finally released. I wasn't exactly sure where I was going with this train of thought, but I was sure that I never wanted to go down the path that I had been on again.

One day, Johnny told me that I should join him in the classes that he was going to in the chapel every Wednesday. The two prison ministers that taught the class were named Jim and Terry. The lessons were about how a man should live as a

Christian. Some of the topics were: sense of self, sense of family, Christians against drug abuse, and several others that I don't remember the names of. All of them though, were news to me. It wasn't that hard for me to get a perfect or near perfect score on the test part of each class. All I had to do was circle the answer that was the opposite of how it had been in my life. I had a lot to learn about being a Christian.

You would think that with all the stuff I was doing that my time would go by fast, but that's just not the case. I was working the breakfast shift in the kitchen, I went to church every night, I went to class every Wednesday, and I did my program class on Friday. Yet, the days still just crept by.

Around the first of November, Johnny and I got word that our jackets had been sent to the Governor's office. She had thirty days to decide if she would sign or not sign. Talk about stress! I was almost to the point where my rubber band was going to break. It's a terrible thing to be counting days when you are locked up, and still not know what the outcome will be at the end of the thirty days. So, I just kept on doing what I did every day. I tried to pay attention to everything but the clock.

It was a Wednesday, and I was in class in the chapel. Jim was teaching the lesson and we were just about to take the test at the end. Suddenly, my cellie appeared in the door way. He motioned for me to come outside and he seemed quite a bit in a hurry. I got up and went outside where my cellie started to tell me to go to my case worker's office because I was going home. He told me that they had already called me three times over the intercom. When I heard this, I freaked out. I ran to his office as fast as I could. When I walked in, he looked up at me and said, "I don't know how you pulled this off, but you are going home in five days."

I was still freaking out, and I was happy! I signed all the papers where he told me to sign, and he shook my hand, telling me congratulations. As soon as I left his office, I ran all the way back to the chapel. I burst into the room and told everyone the good news, then I grabbed Terry and told him to pray for me.

Class was still moving forward, but I couldn't sit still long enough to take my test. I also couldn't leave because the yard was locked down for the count. I bounced from place to place inside the chapel. When the count cleared, Johnny and I went to the smoking area to talk. He was very happy for me, but I know that he was wondering in the back of his mind if he was going to get that same call to come and sign his papers.

There I was, five days left to go, and nothing to do but stare at that clock. I can honestly say that the whole time I was locked up seemed shorter than those last five days. I would check the time and come back two hours later, only to find that only five minutes had passed. Get the picture?

If the clock slowing down wasn't enough, there was the rest of being a short timer to deal with. You see, there are those in prison that will start crap with you just so you won't be able to go home. You have to be very careful to avoid these people. I had done a good job of keeping to myself while I was locked up. I had Johnny, and he had me, but we didn't pal around with many others. Luckily, I didn't have anything that any one wanted, so I got through this as well.

Finally, it was the morning that I was to leave. I went to breakfast with Johnny, and we talked about all the things we had in front of us when he got out. His case worker had told him that he would be out right around Christmas. After breakfast, we smoked a cigarette, and went in for the count. When it cleared, I took my box of clothes and bedding back to the place where they had given them to me. Which left me with nothing but a couple of envelopes and the prison grays that I was wearing. I went to the office at the front of the prison and finished my paper work. They took me to the guard shack that was the way in and out of the prison. I was literally just a few feet from freedom when a strange feeling came over me. I had just realized that I was not going home, but rather, I was just being released.

There was no one that cared that I was about to be free, except for Johnny, and he was still inside.

CHAPTER 32: I WAS FREE, WHICH IS ALSO A FOUR-LETTER WORD

I walked the last few feet to freedom. Once I was through the door, I turned to take one last look at that horrible place that I had made it through. I made up my mind, at that moment, that I would rather be dead than locked up again.

It was December 5, 2011, that my life began again. It was me against the world, with $50 and a ride to Tulsa to start the journey. I liked those odds, because I knew that I could count on me.

I arrived in Tulsa that afternoon. I had paroled to a program named "Wings of Freedom." It was run by a guy named Dixie, who had been in prison himself. He now ran this prison reentry program and he was the pastor of the church that was joined to the program, along with a couple of other businesses. It was quite an operation and it employed several other people, all of whom were retired felons. They were a nice enough group of people   some more than others, but everyone seemed to know their job very well.

They sat me down and got acquainted as they filled out all kinds of paper work on my behalf. When that was finished, they took me to my new digs so that I could get settled in. The whole apartment complex was full of people that were in my same situation. It was like a commune, only we all had our own apartments.

In that program I was expected to get a job and attend four meetings a week. No big deal, except for the curfew, and the fact that I had to take the bus everywhere. The only real hold up was that I wasn't from Tulsa, I was from Oklahoma City. So, I would have to pay attention if I was going to get past these obstacles.

I was settled in, and well on my way, by the time Johnny showed up a couple of weeks later. We were cellies again, only now we called it roommates. It was just like old times except the food was a lot better, and we always made sure there was dessert. We worked well together, Johnny and I, as we figured out how we were going to get through the next couple of years.

We did what was required of us in our program, but we also went to church on Sunday night with Terry, the prison minister that we both knew from the classes that we took while we were locked up. The church he took us to was Park Plaza Church of Christ. It was a large congregation of people and they all seemed really happy to meet us. The night that Johnny and I placed membership was really over the top. After service was over, at least 100 people came over and welcomed us. I was a little overwhelmed by their willingness to accept me, being a convict and all.

It took me a little while to understand that these people were the ones that donated money to the prison ministry that Terry and Jim worked in. They were both full time ministers and these people paid their salary. They were all more than willing to have us as their Christian brothers, regardless of what we had done in the past. I was not used to being around people such as this, and I'll tell you, it was hard for me to understand and accept their friendship. Always

106

in my life, people that were being this nice wanted something from me. I just couldn't figure them out!

CHAPTER 33: JOHNNY WAS A DIVINE INTERVENTION

If you haven't figured out by now why I called Johnny and my friendship a divine intervention, you probably never will. In my mind, though, it was nothing less. We had gone through one of the worst places on earth together, and now we were living life together.

It was just amazing to us both how everything that happened to us seemed to be put in place by God. We landed in the same jail, we were in the same yard, we both got moved to the same place, we both got our sentences reduced, we both made parole in the same month, we both were in the same program, and we both had the same parole officer. So, it should come as no surprise to you that when Park Plaza started a prison reentry program, we both were asked to be the first to join their program. You just can't plan this kind of stuff, it had to be God.

Our parole officer had no problem with us changing to a different program, although he was a little confused at our reason for changing. We told him that we wanted a more interactive and conscientious approach to our program. We wanted to go to the church that we were members of, but most importantly, we needed to be closer to where we were finding all the work we were doing.

There I was, only a few months out of prison and already I was in business for myself. Now this was not part of my original plan, it just ended up that way.

It was at this time that I met Phil. He was really nice to me and went way out of his way to try and help me find a job. He helped me with my resume and even wrote a letter of recommendation, both of which I was to give the man at the interview he had arranged for me. But, even after all of that, I still didn't get that job. Phil asked me what I was going to do and I told him then that I would just work for myself.

Now I don't think that Phil thought that was my best choice at this time in my life, but then he really didn't know what kind of skills I had. Nor did he know what God was planning for me in this part of my life. All I knew was that I had the skills to do whatever the job was, and all I needed was someone to let me show them.

Which brings me to the next good man who God put in my path. His name is Lyle. He had been a contractor for a lot of years, as well as a minister. He was ready to be a full-time minister and leave all that hard work to someone else. So, when he offered me the use of his tools, I was set to do whatever was needed. I can tell you now that if it hadn't been for Lyle, I would never have made it to where I am now.

So, it began. Johnny and I did one job, and then another. Then, those people told someone else, and we did work for them, and so on and so forth. It was slow at first, but by the end of our first year out of prison, we were working pretty steady. Johnny had his driver's license back, and we bought an old truck to work out of. I spent every spare dollar on tools.

Together we just kept moving forward.

CHAPTER 34: SMILE AND SAY "CHEESE"

About two months before I went to prison, I was involved in an accident. I was out delivering my dope to my various customers. I happened to turn down a very dark street and drove right into a huge pothole, which stopped my motorcycle cold and snapped off the front forks. I had gone over the handle bars and landed chin first on the blacktop. My jaw had slammed shut and almost all of my teeth exploded from the impact. Then, the rest of the bike came down and landed on top of me. I was messed up pretty good, but I couldn't stick around for the police or an ambulance.

I called my girlfriend at the house and told her to come and get me, but quick! She was there in only minutes, and I threw the bike in the truck and we took off. She turned the corner just as the ambulance arrived at the scene of the crash. I had gotten away, but I was in bad shape.

The bumps and bruises all healed, but I was left with a mouth full of broken teeth. The whole time I was locked up, I was dealing with the pain of this train wreck in my mouth. The dentist I saw in prison told me that I should get all these broken teeth pulled out and get dentures. He said that these teeth were poisoning me, and that if I didn't do something about it, they might actually kill me.

Now there was one benefit to having been in prison. After you are released on parole, you have free health care for the time you are serving in the free world. This was truly a blessing for me, because

I didn't have to pay a penny to have all my teeth pulled. Each time I went to the dentist, he would pull all the teeth in a quadrant at the same time. Four times I went, and four times he pulled all of them in a quadrant. After my gums had healed I was ready to get my dentures. Except, I had no money to pay for them.

Now you might call this part of what happened, lucky. I, however, call it a blessing from God. Before my gums even had time to heal, a member of Park Plaza walked into the prison ministry office at the church. He just so happened to be a denturist and he wanted to donate a set of dentures as a tithe to God. He was unable to give money, so he gave what he could, a set of teeth. Terry told him that I was just out of prison and that I had just got the last of my teeth pulled so that I could get dentures. He told Terry to bring me by after my gums had finished healing.

I waited about a month and went to see this guy that I didn't even know. He went to work and made me a set of teeth. I went back about a week later and he helped me learn how to put them in and take them out, and how to care for them. I left his office with the biggest smile you can possibly imagine on my face. It actually hurt for me to smile after frowning for so long. But I didn't hurt enough for me to stop doing it. I smiled at everyone I met for a long time after I got those teeth. And to think, they didn't cost me one red cent.

What a gift to give the world! A smile that doesn't cost a thing!

CHAPTER 35: MORE BLESSED THAN I DESERVE!

We have come so far, so fast. It's funny how time flies when you're in the free world. It seemed like I had only been out a week or two, but in reality, it had been a year. I was supposed to do 17 months of parole, but after my 11th month, I had completed all the things I was to do as part of my parole. My Parole Officer told me that if I passed my urinalysis, he was going to cut me loose.

Of course, I passed since I had stayed clean, and he kept his word. I left his office a free man. I cannot find the words to tell you how it felt to be free again. I had beaten a life sentence and lived to tell you about it. The best part was that I was living my new life so much better than I had lived my last one.

It was Jim's wife, Barb, who decided my freedom was in need of celebrating. She and I had grown real close since the first day I met her. What a wonderful woman she was! We would joke all the time about my being her adopted son, but for me it wasn't really a joke. I took it real serious, and cherished every minute that I spent with her. The same thing was true about Judee, only she was my adopted grandmother. What a blessing it was to have such a loving adopted family.

A group of us got together and went out to dinner. There was me of course, and Johnny, Jim and Barb, and Judee and her husband, Bill. You could definitely feel the love in that room, and I took great pleasure in the company that I was keeping.

I had my driver's license back, so I was able to drive again. A license is no big deal until you don't have one. People take for granted their freedom, but not me, I needed that license to live. You see, Johnny and I had graduated from the program at Park Plaza and we now had our own place to live. It was a condo, in a nice part of town. A far cry from our cells in prison.

Work was coming at us faster than we could do it. I had managed to get almost all the tools we needed to work, and what we didn't have, Lyle was still willing to loan me. I had saved up a bunch of money to buy a truck, but hadn't found the one I wanted as of yet.

Johnny and I were also eating really well, and we both had finally gained back all the weight we lost while we were locked up. To say nothing of how dapper we looked in our Sunday-go-to-meeting clothes. Such an improvement over the those grays we wore in prison.

So many blessings had come my way, it's hard to list them all. The only thing left for me to tell you, is something that I just didn't understand at the time. Everywhere I went, the people I encountered told me I was a blessing to them. Now, I liked the way that sounded, but I had no idea how it worked. In my whole life, no one had ever told me I was a blessing to them, until I landed in this group of people that I was involved with. Yes, I still had a lot to learn about being a Christian!

CHAPTER 36: THE ONLY CONSTANT IN THE UNIVERSE IS CHANGE

I was really comfortable in my new life by this point in the story. I had gotten a second chance to live my life, and I was making good use of it. I suppose that is why God chose to shake things up a bit. Most people don't like change because they fear the unknown. I am one of those people.

So, I had known all along that the day would come for Johnny to go home to Oregon, but when it came, I was sad to see him go. I was happy for him to finally be able to get on with his plans for life, but I was sad for me, because I would be left alone to fend for myself.

But one door closes, as another door opens. That is just how God works, don't ask me why! Right after Johnny was gone, it occurred to me that somewhere out there I still had family that cared about me. So, I got on my computer and began to search for them. Trying to find people when you're half way across the country is frustrating . I looked and looked and looked some more, but always came up empty. No one was where they were before I went to prison.

I wrote my mother several letters and all of them went unanswered. They never came back and I never got a reply. My sister was dead, but somewhere out there, her daughter was still alive. Her name was Cortnee, but her whereabout was a mystery to me. I had sent a letter to her at the last address I had, back when Sister was still alive, but I got no reply. And so it went, my search for validation became a very sore subject.

Then someone told me about a website that they had used to find a lost friend. I went home and looked up the site. It was $39.95 to search the unknown on this site, so I paid the money and went on with my search. After hours of looking, I was just about ready to throw in towel. Then, it dawned on me that my stepbrother's name was William, not Bill. I hit search one more time, and there it was, a phone number.

I called the number and Bill answered. We talked a while and he gave me my stepsister's number. When we hung up, I immediately called Peggy, and when she answered I was so excited. We talked for hours as she filled me in on all gossip that pertained to me. Apparently, everyone was so excited to hear from me because they all thought I was dead. It had been nine years since Sister's funeral, and that was the last time anyone had seen me, and if you remember, I had been on a three-day meth binge.

The other good news was that Peggy had Cortnee's number. This was sure good news to me. Cortnee was my last blood relative, so in my mind, she was the most important person for me to find. Don't get me wrong, I loved all the others, but Cortnee was my only link to my baby sister that was no more. I had great hope that Cortnee and I would become as close as her mother and I had been all our lives.

Now finding my family was a real shot in the arm. I was so happy that I told everyone I considered a friend at church what had transpired. It was Phil who seemed to be the happiest for me. So much so, he grabbed his phone and bought me a plane ticket to go and see them at Christmas time. You gotta love Phil! His generosity seems to know no bounds!

This brings me to the last change that I want to tell you about. Jim's wife Barb passed away that year. It was the cancer that killed her body, but her spirit lives on in everyone that knew her. I had gotten so close to her in such a short time. I was devastated when she finally passed away. For months I had gone to see her every Sunday after church. I took her cards, flowers, and stuffed animals to try to bring sunshine into her days, but it was so hard to smile, because you could see the life leaving her every time I went. It was her death that made me understand why people cry at funerals. It's not because they are gone, but rather, it's because you have to go on living without them.

CHAPTER 37: SO MANY BLESSINGS

We are coming to the end of my story. There is not much left to tell you in the way of pivotal moments in life. My life is probably as good as it will get, and that's okay with me. I don't have much to complain about, and that is a good thing! There are just a few things I would like to tell you before we part ways.

God has seen fit to bless me with so many things. My business is doing very well. I have a new helper named Steve, and he has been with me now for almost five years. He is more than just an employee to me, he is a good friend as well. He is the kind of guy that you can trust with everything you own. I enjoy working with him on a daily basis, but more than that, I enjoy giving him a hard time.

Then, there is my family. I have been reunited with all those I care to be. I enjoy my trips to see them each year at Christmas. Mostly because I love them, but any excuse to go to Vegas is a good one!

I moved out of the condo after Johnny left. Now I live in a nice house, on quiet street. I have a big yard for my dog, Bonnie, to play in. She is a good girl and an even better guard dog. I have a cat, too, but what can you say good about a cat? I often sit in my quiet house and think back to those days in prison. I look up and thank God that I am not still there. I would be more than happy to live the rest of my life right here in this house.

I enjoy the fact that I have been sober for over eight years now. I make it a point to celebrate this each year.

God must really have wanted me to survive my beatings, seventeen car wrecks, pistol whippings and stabbings, drug use and prison. I believe he has important things in mind for me to do. Perhaps this book will help lead me to do them by showing at least one person how to overcome a seemingly hopeless situation.

Which brings me to relationships. I am truly blessed to have such a large group of friends. All of them are different in so many ways, but they all bring something with them that brings us close together, as we try to make our way through this cruel world we live in.

I have but one regret to tell you about. I haven't found that special someone to share all of this with, as of yet. But I haven't given up hope either! God gave me a huge heart that is full of love to share. So maybe one day, God willing, I'll tell you the story of how I found true love!

Well, that is all there is! I hope you got something from my story, since I know that I did. I would like remind you that, perfection is a journey, not a destination.

Made in the USA
Monee, IL
29 April 2022